James Moore Swank

Notes and Comments on industrial, economic, political and historical Subjects

James Moore Swank

**Notes and Comments on industrial, economic, political and historical Subjects**

ISBN/EAN: 9783337130329

Printed in Europe, USA, Canada, Australia, Japan

Cover: Foto ©ninafisch / pixelio.de

More available books at **www.hansebooks.com**

# NOTES AND COMMENTS

ON

## INDUSTRIAL, ECONOMIC, POLITICAL, AND HISTORICAL SUBJECTS.

BY

JAMES M. SWANK,

SECRETARY AND GENERAL MANAGER OF THE AMERICAN IRON AND STEEL ASSOCIATION
FROM 1872 TO 1897. AUTHOR OF A HISTORY OF THE MANUFACTURE OF IRON IN
ALL AGES. MEMBER OF THE HISTORICAL SOCIETY OF PENNSYLVANIA.

---

Note it in a book, that it may be for the time to come.—Isaiah xxx. 8.

---

PHILADELPHIA:
THE AMERICAN IRON AND STEEL ASSOCIATION.
1897.

Entered, according to act of Congress, in the year 1897,
BY JAMES M. SWANK,
In the office of the Librarian of Congress, at Washington.

Printed by
ALLEN, LANE & SCOTT,
Nos. 1211-1213 Clover Street,
Philadelphia.

# PREFACE.

THE thirty chapters which compose this volume were not written that they might be gathered into a book. Some of them were written many years ago and others in later years. References to recent events have been added whenever necessary. As the editor of the publications of the American Iron and Steel Association during the last twenty-five years it has been my duty and pleasure to present to the readers of these publications industrial, economic, and other facts of special interest, and to accompany them with such comments as seemed to be pertinent and necessary. The chapters which are bound up in the present volume have been selected from these editorial contributions. In making these selections I have confined them in the main to such subjects as are likely to possess present interest for students of our industrial and economic history. The few concluding chapters which do not relate to these subjects are added because, alike with the chapters which precede them, they are relevant to that revival of interest in every phase of American history which is now everywhere so apparent. Many chapters necessarily embody only introductory and suggestive comments on the subjects to which they relate.

The creeds of political parties in our country have long expressed directly opposite views concerning the best methods of promoting our industrial prosperity, one party believing in the fostering influence of tariff legislation and the other party opposing this policy. In several of the chapters which follow I have recorded the results of these conflicting policies. First, however, considerable space has been devoted to the experience of Great Britain in building up its industries by protective duties and through other measures resting for support directly upon the British Government. The industrial history of our own country can not be even briefly summarized without reference to that of the mother country, Great Britain having constantly sought to control our industrial development from colonial times to the present time. Mention of the industrial policy of Great Britain in these pages has also been necessary because of the prevalence in our own country during the greater part of our national existence of a formidable political sentiment that is favorable to the present British policy of free trade. The British theories underlying the Wilson tariff of 1894 were precisely the same as those upon which the Walker tariff of 1846 was based. In fifty years this country had moved in a cycle of so-called political economy and had apparently learned nothing.

American workingmen may well study the treatment that the workingmen of Great Britain have usually received from their employers and from the aristocratic classes. In two of the chapters of this volume I have only touched upon this great subject. Those who would know more of the hard life of British toilers should read chapters 5 and 16 of *Fifty Years Ago*, by Walter Besant, published in 1888 ; *In Darkest England*, by General Booth, published in 1890 ; *Masses and Classes*, by Henry Tuckley, published in 1893 ; and *The White Slaves of England*, by Robert H. Sherard, published in 1897. These are all recent publications. Saddest of all let them read the fulsome dispatches from London during the Queen's Jubilee, in June last, which told of the dinner given by the Princess of Wales to the poor of that city. "*About three hundred thousand denizens of the slums were sumptuously entertained.*" This was in the Queen's capital in 1897. We do not want British industrial conditions in our country.

The discontent with existing conditions which has so widely prevailed in our own country in recent years, the practically unrestricted immigration of foreigners into our country, the necessity for establishing steamship lines to all parts of the world, and the mistaken policy of reciprocity are subjects of present interest to which a few chapters of this book are devoted.

No. 261 SOUTH FOURTH STREET, PHILADELPHIA, December 31, 1897.

# CONTENTS.

## CHAPTER I.
### ENGLAND ONCE THE INDUSTRIAL SERVANT OF OTHER COUNTRIES.

England almost entirely an agricultural country down to the 16th century—For centuries foreign merchants ruled the trade of England absolutely—Other countries supplied her with manufactured goods—Even English agriculture did not flourish—Poverty of the English people while their energies were chiefly devoted to agriculture..................Pages 1-7

## CHAPTER II.
### BRITISH INDUSTRIES DEVELOPED BY PROTECTION.

England began in a feeble way to diversify her industries by protective duties in the 14th century—Application of the protective policy long limited to the crudest English products—In the 15th and 16th centuries legislation for the benefit of English industries gradually grew more restrictive and effective—But it was not until Queen Elizabeth's reign (1558-1603) that England became a leading manufacturing and commercial nation—England now began to seek foreign markets for the sale of her finished products—Under Cromwell the protective policy was further extended, and by means of the navigation acts of his time the foreign trade of England was greatly enlarged—Blackstone's account of England's protective policy—Her protective policy became a prohibitory policy in the 18th century—The protective policy still apparent in British steamship subsidies ................................................................ Pages 8-22

## CHAPTER III.
### THE BRITISH WORKINGMAN UNDER VICTORIA AND HER IMMEDIATE PREDECESSORS.

The Jubilee of Queen Victoria in 1897—The prosperity of Great Britain during her long reign due largely to the extension of the foreign trade of that country—Warlike spirit of British manufacturing and commercial competition—Effect of the fierceness of this competition upon British workingmen and their families—Efforts of British workingmen to better their condition always opposed by the ruling classes of Great Britain—Some examples of this policy—British workingmen systematically underpaid and degraded that British goods may be cheaply produced—Testimony upon this subject of various English writers.............Pages 23-33

## CHAPTER IV.
### THE HOPELESS POOR OF GREAT BRITAIN.

England under Queen Victoria not merry with the daily life of her working people—Testimony of Professor James E. Thorold Rogers, Sir Edward Sullivan, Dr. Edward Young, Hon. William E. Dodge, Benjamin Disraeli, General William Booth, and others; also of several leading English newspapers—Destitution and wretchedness of the London poor—Pitiable condition of women and children in Great Britain who are poor....Pages 34-47

## CHAPTER V.
### THE BRITISH POLICY OF FREE TRADE.

Mr. Gladstone's claim that free trade has improved the wages of British workingmen refuted by the Sheffield Telegraph and the London Times—Testimony of Charles Kingsley and Cardinal Manning concerning the ill results of the teachings of the Manchester school—British agriculture not prosperous under free trade—True causes of the improvement in the wages of British workingmen—Mr. Gladstone a poor prophet......Pages 48-53

## CHAPTER VI.
### THE DESTRUCTION OF IRISH MANUFACTURES.

Irish industries systematically repressed and stamped out by England—Mr. Commissioner Mac Carthy, Edmund Burke, and Dean Swift tell how their destruction was accomplished—William Cobbett and Judge Byles explain the consequences—Futile protests by both houses of the Irish Parliament against the withdrawal of protection from Irish industries by the Act of Union of 1801—Remarkable decline in the population of Ireland from 1841 to 1891—Further proofs by Thomas Francis Meagher and Professor Robert Ellis Thompson of the destruction of Irish manufactures........Pages 54-60

## CHAPTER VII.
### AN IMPERIAL BRITISH ZOLLVEREIN.

Free trade not popular with all classes in Great Britain—The proposed British zollverein, or customs-union, a protective movement—Reasons why the scheme will not succeed........................................................Pages 61-64

## CHAPTER VIII.
### BRITISH STEAMSHIP SUBSIDIES.

Great Britain's enormous annual subsidies to steamship companies—Judge Kelley and John Roach, also the Glasgow Herald and the London Engineering, cite the proofs of the payments of these subsidies—Colonel William F. Prosser explains the benefits of steamship subsidies to British trade—List of European subsidized steamship companies in 1896—The United States should also adopt the policy of subsidizing steamship lines to all parts of the world..............................................................Pages 65-69

CONTENTS. vii

## CHAPTER IX.
### TARIFF LEGISLATION FROM WASHINGTON TO McKINLEY.

The protective policy approved by the founders of our Government—The protection of American labor one of the reasons for the adoption of the Constitution of 1787—Our first tariff act was a measure of protection—Alexander Hamilton's masterly report in 1791 in support of a protective policy—Senator John P. Jones's philosophical speech in 1890 a worthy companion of Hamilton's report—The Morrill tariff of 1861 the first in a long series of protective tariff enactments extending to 1894—The Dingley tariff of 1897 a thoroughly protective measure..................................................Pages 70-82

## CHAPTER X.
### THE TARIFFS OF 1842, 1846, AND 1857.

President Tyler's tribute to the beneficial effects of the protective tariff of 1842—Injurious effects of the revenue tariff of 1846 upon our iron industry—Testimony of Cooper & Hewitt—Statement by W. J. Parsons—Testimony of Professor Francis Bowen—Evil results of ad valorem duties illustrated by citations of iron prices—Extract from President Fillmore's message in 1852—The hard times of 1855—Extract from the New York Tribune—The disastrous consequences of the revenue tariff of 1857—Extract from the Boston Sentinel—Testimony of Judge Kelley.................................Pages 83-92

## CHAPTER XI.
### TARIFF LEGISLATION FROM 1870 TO 1897.

The Schenck tariff bill of 1870—The Morrison tariff bill of 1876 not considered by the House—The Wood tariff bill of 1878 defeated—The Covert steel-rail bill of 1880 defeated in the Ways and Means Committee—The Tariff Commission of 1882—The tariff of 1883—Mr. Morrison's horizontal reduction tariff bill of 1884 defeated—President Cleveland, in his first annual message, in 1885, recommends a reduction of duties—Mr. Morrison introduces early in 1886 another tariff bill, which is defeated—Mr. Morrison introduces late in 1886 still another bill proposing a reduction of duties, which is also defeated—In December, 1887, President Cleveland sends to Congress his celebrated message again recommending a reduction of duties—Mr. Mills introduces a tariff reduction bill in 1888, which passed the House but did not pass the Senate—The Senate protective tariff bill of 1888 passed by that body in 1889, but not considered by the House—The McKinley protective tariff of 1890—The Wilson revenue tariff of 1894—The Dingley protective tariff of 1897........................Pages 93-106

## CHAPTER XII.
### ALEXANDER HAMILTON.

Hamilton's unanswerable report in favor of protection—Philadelphia, in which city it was written, the foremost protectionist city in the Union—Hamilton's memory not sufficiently honored.........................Pages 107-108

## CHAPTER XIII.

### TARIFF CONVENTIONS IN THE OLDEN TIME.

A national tariff convention at Harrisburg, Pennsylvania, in 1827—A national tariff convention at New York in 1831—Two conventions of iron manufacturers in 1849, one at Pittsburgh and another at Philadelphia, called to protest against the tariff of 1846—A national tariff convention at New York in 1881—Organization of the American Iron Association in 1855 and of the American Iron and Steel Association in 1864..............Pages 109–117

## CHAPTER XIV.

### WHY THE SOUTHERN CONFEDERACY FAILED.

Provision in the Constitution of the Confederate States prohibiting protective duties—The South seceded partly to establish free trade—Testimony of Congressman George D. Tillman, of South Carolina—The New Orleans Daily City Item discusses the economic conditions of the Confederacy—General Richard Taylor, of Louisiana, pays a tribute to the superior economic conditions of the Northern States—The South now diversifying its industries..................................................................Pages 118–120

## CHAPTER XV.

### PROTECTION IS NOT MONOPOLY.

Monopolies not necessarily evils—Examples of beneficial monopolies—Monopolies not created by protection—They exist in free trade England—A monopoly which was long maintained by the American Congress for the exclusive benefit of foreign manufacturers..................................Pages 121–124

## CHAPTER XVI.

### ABANDONED NEW ENGLAND FARMS.

Farms in New England not abandoned because protection is hostile to agriculture—Notable testimony in an address in 1857 or 1858 that New England farms were then abandoned.............................................Pages 125–127

## CHAPTER XVII.

### CHEAPENING THE NECESSARIES OF LIFE.

Selfishness and the free trader becloud the question of cheap prices—The free trader endeavors to set class against class—Cheapness that may be obtained without degrading labor—This kind of cheapness the result of protection—Cheapness not the chief good................................Pages 128–131

## CHAPTER XVIII.

### CAPITAL THE FRIEND OF LABOR.

Henry C. Carey's favorite quotation—A paraphrase for the consideration of American workingmen—The more capital the more employment for labor—Most of our rich men were once poor men......................Pages 132–136

CONTENTS. ix

## CHAPTER XIX.
### OUR COLONIAL IRON INDUSTRY.
Beginning of our colonial iron industry in Virginia and Massachusetts—The ancestors of Washington and Lincoln were ironmakers, as were also several of the noted men of the Revolutionary period—Statistics of our colonial iron industry—England discouraged the manufacture of iron in the colonies—Influences which retarded the development of the iron industry in Virginia and stimulated the industry in other colonies—Characteristics of our colonial iron industry—The decline of the iron industry in New England and in North and South Carolina—New York and New Jersey not maintaining their colonial prestige..............Pages 137-144

## CHAPTER XX.
### REMARKABLE DEVELOPMENT OF OUR IRON AND STEEL INDUSTRIES SINCE 1860.
An era of great activity and unexampled progress in these industries opened with the enactment of the Morrill tariff in 1861 and the beginning of our civil war—Summary of this progress from 1861 to 1897 in the various branches of production—Old methods of manufacture abandoned—"How far is it to the next forge?"—All iron and steel products greatly cheapened since 1861—Phenomenal reduction in the prices of steel rails—Railroads great consumers of iron and steel—The United States leads the world in the production of iron and steel—The census of 1890 shows how great is the investment of capital and how large the number of workmen employed and the wages paid in our iron and steel industries—Depression in these industries in 1893 and 1894 and again in 1896 and the early part of 1897—The future of these industries..........Pages 145-159

## CHAPTER XXI.
### REVELATIONS OF AN OLD LEDGER.
An iron town in Pennsylvania early in the nineteenth century—Primitive methods of transportation—Colonial methods of bookkeeping—Pounds, shillings, and pence—Tons, hundredweights, quarters, and pounds—Early forges and an early furnace in the Alleghenies...................Pages 160-166

## CHAPTER XXII.
### THE EARLY HISTORY OF PITTSBURGH.
Pittsburgh the centre of the iron, steel, bituminous coal, and glass industries of the world—The site of Fort Pitt selected in 1753 by Washington—His prominent part in the military operations at Pittsburgh and in its vicinity which resulted in driving the French from the Ohio Valley in 1758—His first and only surrender—The important battle of Bushy Run—Washington's last visit to Pittsburgh in 1770—Leading events in the early history of Pittsburgh—Development of its coal and iron industries—Its present prominence—"The State of Allegheny"...................Pages 167-176

## CHAPTER XXIII.
### THE RESTRICTION OF IMMIGRATION.

Statistics of immigration from 1789 to 1896—Beginning of the great flood of immigration dates from 1845—Causes which influenced the heavy immigration half a century ago—Comparatively few immigrants from Italy or the Slavic countries of Europe prior to 1876—Large arrivals since that year—Statistics of Chinese immigration from 1853 to 1888—Opposition to immigration dates from about 1844—Government action directly responsible for unrestricted and excessive immigration..................Pages 177-183

## CHAPTER XXIV.
### THE DRIFT OF POPULATION TO THE GREAT CITIES.

Census statistics of urban and rural population—City advantages now possessed by the country and by country towns—Farmers are large gainers by the progressive ideas of the last fifty years......................Pages 184-188

## CHAPTER XXV.
### THE WESTERN FARMERS' DISCONTENT.

The discontent of Western farmers the result of causes beyond anybody's control—Western farmers not discriminated against in tariff or other legislation—The homestead law—Government land grants to Western railroad companies—The Department of Agriculture established for the benefit of farmers—Agricultural colleges established and endowed by grants of public lands—The interstate commerce law enacted at the request of farmers—Tariff legislation for their special benefit—The real cause of hard times for Western farmers........................Pages 189-194

## CHAPTER XXVI.
### HISTORY OF RECIPROCITY LEGISLATION.

History of the insertion of the reciprocity policy in the McKinley tariff of 1890—The sugar bounty provision of that act an entirely new feature in our tariff legislation—Fishing bounties—A sugar bounty never approved in a Republican national platform—Reciprocity treaties with Canada and Hawaii—Revenue lost under the reciprocity treaties negotiated under the tariff act of 1890—Our exports of iron and steel not helped by reciprocity—Reciprocity in the Dingley tariff—Our experience with Canadian reciprocity described by Senator Morrill.............................Pages 195-201

## CHAPTER XXVII.
### HOW SCHUYLER COLFAX ROSE TO BE VICE PRESIDENT.

The House of Representatives has had two Speakers who were editors by profession, Schuyler Colfax and James G. Blaine—Dinner in honor of Mr. Colfax's election to the Speakership in 1863—Address of Samuel Wilkeson—"Folks depend on him"—Secret of Mr. Colfax's success......Pages 202-205

## CHAPTER XXVIII.
### BUCKEYES IN AMERICAN HISTORY.

Virginia and Ohio most prominent of all the States in furnishing the country with distinguished men—Since the surrender at Appomattox Virginia has lost her ancient prestige in this particular—Ohio has never relaxed her efforts in this direction since her admission into the Union in 1803—List of Ohio's most prominent civilians, including four Presidents and two others born within her borders—List of Ohio's most prominent military heroes, including Grant, Sherman, and Sheridan—List of Ohio's prominent literary men and women..............................................................Pages 206-210

## CHAPTER XXIX.
### OUR NEARNESS TO REVOLUTIONARY TIMES.

It is only a little over a hundred years since Washington's inauguration—Many persons now living have known Revolutionary soldiers—Lafayette died as late as 1834—Two Presidents, Jackson and John Quincy Adams, who were born in 1767, lived to 1845 and 1848 respectively—Charles Carroll of Carrollton, one of the signers of the Declaration of Independence, lived until 1832—Notable Philadelphians who have known Revolutionary heroes—Richard W. Thompson, who is still living at Terre Haute, can describe the personal appearance of Jefferson and Madison, who were born in 1743 and 1749 respectively—Senator Morrill can describe the personal appearance of Monroe and Judge Paine, and Frederick Fraley can describe the personal appearance of Monroe and Chief Justice Marshall—Looking backward one hundred and fifty years....................Pages 211-217

## CHAPTER XXX.
### HONORING THE MIGHTY DEAD.

Notable address of ex-Minister Edward J. Phelps in 1891—Our country's great men are fitly honored—Conspicuous examples of the honors that have been paid to our deceased heroes and sages—Bancroft's eulogy of Lincoln and Blaine's eulogy of Garfield contrasted—Blaine's eloquent words in closing his eulogy of Garfield—A remarkable peroration—Harrison's unequaled eulogy of Grant............................................................Pages 218-223

# CHAPTER I.

ENGLAND ONCE THE INDUSTRIAL SERVANT OF OTHER COUNTRIES.

UNTIL in very recent years British writers on free trade never tired in commending to the people of the United States the policy of devoting their energies mainly to agriculture, as if they had just been emancipated from barbarism and possessed no higher capabilities and no other resources than those which pertain to the most primitive of all occupations. The motive in giving this advice was, however, not past finding out. The Birmingham *Gazette* remarked in 1875: "While England and America are in a great measure one in language, literature, laws, arts, and religion, *the mercantile interests of the two nations are not identical.*" The *Gazette* and other organs of British public opinion did not want the mercantile interests of the two countries to be identical; their policy and that of the British Government has always been the suppression of all American industries except agriculture.

When we were still British colonies the first Lord Sheffield declared that "*the only use* and advantage of American colonies or West India islands is the monopoly of their consumption and the carriage of their produce." Bancroft says that "England, in its relations with other States, sought a convenient tariff; *in the colonies it prohibited industry.*" In 1816 Lord Brougham, in a speech in Parliament advocating the increased exportation of British goods to the

United States, declared that "it was well worth while to incur a loss upon the first exportation, in order by the glut to *stifle in the cradle* those rising manufactures in the United States which the war has forced into existence contrary to the natural course of things." Mr. Robinson, a member of Parliament, said in a memorable speech quoted by Henry Clay in 1832: "Other nations knew, as well as the noble lord opposite and those who acted with him, what we meant by free trade was nothing more nor less than, by means of the great advantages we enjoyed, to get a *monopoly* of all their markets for our manufactures, and to prevent them, one and all, from ever becoming manufacturing nations." In 1843 the London *Spectator* said: "More general considerations tend to show that the trade between the two countries, most beneficial to both, must be what is commonly called *a colonial trade;* the new-settled country importing the manufactures of the old in exchange for *its own raw produce.* In all economical relations the United States still stand to England in the relation of *colony to mother country.*"

By the help of our policy of protection to home industries the United States is now fully abreast of Great Britain as a manufacturing country, and the advice of British writers to confine our energies to agriculture has given way to serious apprehension concerning the manufacturing and commercial prosperity of their own country, Continental and American manufacturers having successfully invaded the home markets of the United Kingdom, as well as those colonial and other markets which British manufacturers once regarded as their exclusive possession.

England, always the greater part of Great Britain, once pursued the unwise policy her free traders have commended to us. This was particularly so from the twelfth century to the sixteenth century, when all England was almost entirely an agricultural country, her people being chiefly supplied with manufactured goods by enterprising merchants from other countries, who employed the vessels of these countries in making their exchanges. "Even iron was imported from the Continent for the use of English blacksmiths." In commercial and manufacturing enterprise England was greatly excelled down to the sixteenth century by the powerful cities of Italy, Spain, Germany, and the Netherlands, while Portugal and France were fairly her rivals. Commerce and manufactures were so little understood by the people of England in the thirteenth century that important concessions were made by the government to the powerful merchants of the Hanseatic League to induce them to settle in England, with permission to manufacture abroad the goods that the English people would buy. For a hundred years this great corporation engrossed almost the whole of the foreign trade of England, using its own shipping and furnishing employment to its own factories on the Continent; and for three hundred years, down to the reign of Queen Elizabeth, it was a powerful competitor with other foreigners and with native Englishmen for the possession of that trade. Foreign merchants ruled the trade of England absolutely down to the sixteenth century. In 1483 an English statute referred to the "merchant strangers of the nation of Italy, who bring and convey from the parts beyond sea great substance of wares and merchandises . . at their pleasure and there sell the same as well by retail as otherwise."

The manufactured goods with which the people of England were supplied by foreign merchants were largely paid for with the raw products of English farms and mines and with the fish caught upon English coasts. Macpherson, in his *Annals of Commerce*, states that, in the fourteenth century, "England imported none of the raw materials for manufactures which are so largely imported into Great Britain to-day, while her exports consisted almost entirely of the most valuable raw materials, and of cloths in an unfinished state, which may also be classed among raw materials." The land was also drained of its precious metals. In the fifteenth century a commercial writer complained that the foreigners " bear the gold out of this land, and suck the thrift out of our hand, as the wasp sucketh honey out of the bee." Wool was a principal article of export in the thirteenth and fourteenth centuries. "Raising and spreading a story that wool would not be suffered to be exported in such a year . . was, on account of its being an injury to trade, punished by indictment." The Flemish woolen manufacturers, who bought English wool, had attained such prominence in the thirteenth century and their products such celebrity that an old writer declared that "all the world was clothed in English wool wrought by the Flemish weavers." Foreigners manufactured English wool and finished English woolen cloths and sold them back to England with a profit. It was this condition of affairs that gave rise to the proverb: "The stranger buys of the Englishman the fox's skin for a groat and sells him the tail for a shilling."

While England was thus limiting her energies to a rude agriculture and to the exportation of raw products it is recorded that the manufactures of Florence were a source of great profit to its people. "Two hundred establishments, with thirty thousand workmen, were employed in the manufacture of wool." At Bruges, in Flanders, "the merchants of seventeen kingdoms had their factories and domiciles, beside many from almost unknown lands who flocked within its walls." Bruges was a great manufacturing and commercial emporium. "While the merchant frequented the mart the weaver was busy at his loom, in the production of silk and linen fabrics, as well as woolen cloths."

For hundreds of years after the revival of trade and commerce on the Continent of Europe which followed the beginning of the Crusades in the eleventh century England pursued in the main the losing policy we have briefly sketched. Strangers manufactured for her, acted as her merchants in her large cities, and filled her ports with their ships. Neither her commerce nor her manufactures flourished, nor did her agriculture. The last was of the most primitive and wasteful kind and was far surpassed by that of Italy and the Netherlands. The agriculture of these countries had been greatly benefited by the attention paid to commerce and manufactures. That of Italy was worthy of comparison with the best results of the nineteenth century. "The Netherlands, too, once covered with swamps and forests, became a rich agricultural country; farms and gardens surrounded the manufactory and the mart; and the wain richly laden with the treasures of merchandise, as it slowly traversed the roads of Brabant, passed through a rich country, where the mower filled his hand and he that bound sheaves his bosom." But in England "the tillage of fields was very imperfect, producing extremely scanty crops; the implements of husbandry were rude; oxen were so badly fed that it required six of them to draw a plow, which barely turned up half an acre in a summer's day. . . . As there was so little inclosed meadow land, as the cultivation of artificial grasses and turnips was unknown, winter provender for cattle was very scarce; hence many were killed before they were fat." In 1563 a royal decree was issued abolishing the "bloomeries," or "iron smithies," in Furness in Lancashire, in compliance with a petition of the inhabitants, "because they consumed all the loppings and croppings, the sole winter food for their cattle." "Vegetables were scarce. The roots that now smoke on our table, cabbages, carrots, and potatoes, were unknown in England." The harvests frequently failed and great suffering followed. "As late as 1547 bullocks bought for the navy weighed less than four hundred pounds." The agriculture of England, like her manufactures, has attained its highest development in the eighteenth and nineteenth centuries, but it is not to-day as prosperous as it has been.

It can not be said that the English people were prosperous while agriculture was almost their sole occupation. The masses certainly were not. In the thirteenth and fourteenth centuries "the purchase of a pound of candles would have almost absorbed a workman's daily wages. Few persons could have afforded to break the curfew." Clothing was so dear that ordinary linen shirts were devised by will from one generation to another. Even among the upper classes "the cloak, robe, or gown of the day was often the coverlet at night." Glass windows were practically unknown in the huts of the lower classes. "The sale of wool and woolfels was the chief profit of the farmer," so little did he diversify his crops. Among the masses "the pig was the most important article of diet," and "during half the year salted meat and hard fish formed the subsistence of the greater part of the community." Iron was dear and nearly all of it was imported. Metal vessels for domestic use were real luxuries. In the thirteenth and fourteenth centuries iron for the tires of wagons and carts was so dear in England that many wheels were not ironed, and iron teeth for English harrows were unknown. Hallam expresses the opinion that in the fourteenth century the middle classes of Italy were much more comfortable than those of France or England. The people of the Netherlands also at that period possessed more of the comforts of civilization than the people of England. In the fifteenth and sixteenth centuries the houses of the working people of England were still bare of simple comforts and conveniences. "There were very few chimneys even in capital towns; the fire was laid to the wall, and the smoke issued out at the roof or door or window. The houses were wattled and plastered over with clay, and all the furniture and utensils were of wood. The people slept on straw pallets, with a log of wood for a pillow." In the sixteenth century carpets were unknown in England, and the floor of the royal presence chamber of Queen Mary and Queen Elizabeth was covered with rushes or hay.

There is abundant evidence of the fact that, down to the sixteenth century, absorbing devotion to agriculture, with corresponding neglect of manufacturing and commercial pursuits, improved neither the agriculture nor the people of England. In the five hundred years from 1075 to 1575 the population of England and Wales but little more than doubled. We can easily imagine what would be the condition of that agriculture and of that people to-day if the policy which so long made England the industrial follower instead of the industrial leader of nations had been continued.

# CHAPTER II.

### BRITISH INDUSTRIES DEVELOPED BY PROTECTION.

RESTRICTIVE legislation concerning the exportation of wool and the importation of woolen cloths was adopted by England early in the reign of Edward III., in the first half of the fourteenth century. Sir William Blackstone remarks of the legislation in the reign of Edward: "Much also was done, under the auspices of this magnanimous prince, for establishing our domestic manufactures by *prohibiting* the exportation of English wool and the importation or *wear* of foreign cloth or furs, and by encouraging clothworkers from other countries to settle here." From Edward's time the protective policy is clearly marked in English history, although its application was long limited to the crudest industries. Nor was it persistently adhered to by some of Edward's immediate successors. At first only the manufacture of common woolen goods was made the subject of protective legislation; the Continent still continued without restriction to supply fine cloths, tapestries, silks, linens, laces, cutlery, iron, etc., for many years. Nor did the exportation of wool come to an end; it "became a monopoly of the king's exchequer."

In the fifteenth and sixteenth centuries the legislation of England affecting the importation of foreign goods competing with those of domestic manufacture, or retarding domestic manufacturing enterprise, gradually grew more and more restrictive. Under Edward IV., in the fifteenth century, the importation of many manufactured articles was entirely prohibited. When Queen Elizabeth was upon the throne, during the latter part of the sixteenth century, the effect of this policy, of which she was an ardent advocate, was seen in the steady development of the manufacturing and commercial interests of the kingdom. Then, for the first time, England began to manifest the possession of those wonderful capabilities which have made her the first commercial and manufacturing nation of modern times.

The policy of Edward III., which gave England her start in many important branches of manufactures, was cotemporaneous with the settlement in the country of some Flemish weavers. Others of their countrymen accepted the inducements to immigration which were offered by Edward, and still other skilled foreigners followed the Flemish workmen. In time, however, the large number of foreign artisans who had settled in England excited the jealousy of native manufacturers, and in the early part of the sixteenth century many thousand Belgians were expelled from the country by Henry VIII. A few years after the expulsion of the Belgians summary measures were successfully resorted to by Elizabeth to rid England of the ships and merchandise of the powerful Hanseatic League, which for centuries had enjoyed Parliamentary privileges amounting almost to a monopoly of English commerce. Henry's and Elizabeth's acts were measures of the most radical *protection*, as were those previous enactments which had prohibited the importation of foreign goods. English statesmanship and philanthropy first invited foreign merchants and skilled workmen to cultivate intimate relations with the unskilled people of England, and then, when the lessons so greatly needed had been freely imparted, they were informed that their services were no longer required and that their company was not wanted.

Elizabeth was, however, in one respect wiser than Henry. She did not banish from England skilled workmen of foreign birth who had sought her shores. She encouraged the immigration of Huguenot refugees which had commenced a few years before her accession to the throne, and partly in consequence of this encouragement her reign, as already intimated, was a prosperous one for her people. The Huguenots brought over from France the knowledge of many of the mechanic arts of which England had previously been ignorant. "In 1560 a pair of black silk stockings, knit in England, was presented to Queen Elizabeth" as a great achievement. In the closing years of the seventeenth century, after the revocation of the edict of Nantes in 1685, the accession to her population of other Huguenot refugees still further added to the manufacturing skill and developed the manufacturing resources of England. Soon after the middle of the sixteenth century numerous German miners and smelters were induced by Elizabeth to settle in England. Special privileges were granted to companies of English merchants and vessel owners during the reign of Elizabeth, and this policy proved to be a most efficient means of affording encouragement and protection to the manufacturing as well as to the commercial interests of England.

The protective measures we have recited had encouraged the merchants of England to seek foreign markets to exchange English products for the products of other countries, and at the close of the sixteenth century and the beginning of the seventeenth century English manufactures had obtained an entrance into the world's markets. Employment was thus found for English shipbuilders and English sailors, as well as for English weavers and other English mechanics.

Yet England needed to take one step more to assure the continued growth of her foreign trade. Most of this trade was still conducted in foreign vessels. "Even the produce of the British colonies was brought to England in Dutch bottoms." The important step was taken in the passage of the navigation acts in Cromwell's time, about the middle of the seventeenth century. Judge William D. Kelley says of England's navigation acts under Cromwell: "She legislated in favor of her own ships. The foreign article brought in English bottoms came into her ports under differential duties lower than those on the same article coming in on the same day in foreign bottoms. She thus stimulated the building of English ships and created a great English navy." The importation of colonial products in any other than English ships was prohibited. The navigation acts of the Cromwellian Protectorate were supplemented by others of similar character in the reign of Charles II. and afterwards.

All these acts were measures of real protection to English trade, as much so as were the laws previously passed to encourage home manufactures and the sale of their products in foreign markets.

The navigation acts of Great Britain were greatly modified in 1849 and in subsequent years. Foreign ships were permitted without restriction to carry foreign merchandise to British ports and to receive return cargoes. Ships not of British build were permitted to be registered as British ships and bear the British flag if wholly owned by British subjects. The first concession was made to aid in the extension of British trade, and the second signified nothing, for it had been demonstrated that British-built ships were as cheap as any that could be bought.

Further details of the protection afforded by acts of Parliament to English industries are instructive. As one result of the Huguenot immigration into England the manufacture of silk was greatly extended. "To cherish the industry the duties on imported silks were *trebled* and then their importation *prohibited.*" In 1678 an act was passed for the encouragement of the woolen industry which required that "all dead bodies should be wrapped in woolen shrouds." This act remained in force until 1808. The Irish linen manufacture was established through liberal grants from William of Orange and succeeding sovereigns. The fisheries of Scotland were built up by government bounties.

Blackstone, in his chapter on "offenses against public trade," states that "owling, . . the offense of transporting wool or sheep out of this kingdom, to the detriment of its staple manufacture, . . was forbidden at common law . . and by many later statutes. The statute 8 Elizabeth, c. 3, makes the transportation of live sheep, or embarking them on board any ship, for the first offense forfeiture of goods and imprisonment for a year, and at the end of the year the left hand shall be cut off in some public market, and shall be there nailed up in the openest place; and the second offense is felony"—that is, death. "The statutes 12 Charles II., c. 3, and 7 and 8 William III., c. 28, . . make the exportation of wool, sheep, or fuller's earth liable to pecuniary penalties, and the forfeiture of the interest of the ship and cargo by the owners, if privy, and confiscation of goods, and three years' imprisonment to the master and all the mariners;" and the statutes 4 George I. and 12 and

19 George II. "make it transportation for seven years if the penalties be not paid." These prohibitions of the exportation of wool, sheep, and fuller's clay were not repealed until the present century.

The same distinguished author, in the same chapter, records another restriction upon the freedom of trade which was enforced during the eighteenth century and repealed only after its close: "*To prevent the destruction of our home manufactures by transporting and seducing our artists to settle abroad* it is provided, by statute 5 George I., c. 27, that such as so entice or seduce them shall be fined £100 and be imprisoned three months; and for the second offense shall be fined at discretion and be imprisoned a year; and the artificers so going into foreign countries, and not returning within six months after warning given them by the British ambassador where they reside, shall be deemed aliens and forfeit all their land and goods, and shall be incapable of any legacy or gift. By statute 23 George II., c. 13, the seducers incur, for the first offense, a forfeiture of £500 for each artificer contracted with to be sent abroad and imprisonment for twelve months; and for the second, £1,000, and are liable to two years' imprisonment; and, by the same statute, connected with 14 George III., c. 71, if any person exports any tools or utensils used in the silk, linen, cotton, or woolen manufactures, (excepting wool cards to North America,) he forfeits the same and £200, and the captain of the ship (having knowledge thereof) £100; and if any captain of a king's ship, or officer of the customs, knowingly suffers such exportation he forfeits £100 and his employment, and is forever made incapable of bearing any public office; and every person collecting such tools or utensils in order to export the same shall, on conviction at the assizes, forfeit such tools and also £200." In 1825 and again in 1833 the exportation of machinery for the manufacture of cotton, woolen, linen, and silk goods was again *prohibited*. It was not permitted to be exported until 1845.

Near the close of the seventeenth century, in the reign of William III., the exportation of frames or engines for knitting gloves or stockings was prohibited under heavy penalties. A hundred years later, in 1782, "a special act was passed, prohibiting the exportation of engraved copper-plates and blocks, or enticing any workmen employed in printing calicoes to go beyond the sea, under the penalty of £500 and twelve months' imprisonment." The statutes prohibiting artificers from going abroad were not finally repealed until 1825.

The acts of Parliament above recited were of general and universal application, and, in the language of Sir William Blackstone, already quoted, were intended "to prevent the destruction of our home manufactures"—more properly to promote their development and growth. The restrictions which the mother country saw fit to impose on her North American colonies were, however, equally as severe as those general prohibitions and penalties which have been quoted. Dr. William Elder states the character of these restrictions as follows: "The colonies were held under restraint so absolute that, beyond the common domestic industries, and the most ordinary mechanical employments, no kind of manufactures was permitted. In 1750 a hatter-shop in Massachusetts was declared a nuisance by the British Parliament. In the same year an act was passed permitting the importation of pig iron from the colonies, because charcoal, then exclusively employed in smelting the ore, was well-nigh exhausted in England; but forbidding the erection of tilt-hammers, slitting or rolling mills, or any establishment for the manufacture of steel." A law of Virginia, passed in 1684, to encourage textile manufactures in that province, was annulled in England. Lord Chatham declared that "the British colonists of North America had no *right* to manufacture even a nail for a horseshoe." From 1719 to 1732 British merchants "complained in memorials to the government that the people of Massachusetts, New York, Connecticut, Rhode Island, and Maryland were setting up manufactures of woolen and linen for the use of their own families, and of flax and hemp for coarse bags and halters." McCulloch, in his *Commercial Dictionary*, declares that "it was also a leading principle in the system of colonial policy, adopted as well by England as by the other European nations, to discourage all attempts to manufacture such articles in the colonies as could be provided for them by the mother country."

The act of Parliament concerning the manufacture of iron in the colonies, above alluded to, was passed in the twenty-third year of the reign of George II., and printed in pamphlet form in 1750 by Thomas Baskett, of London, "Printer to the King's Most Excellent Majesty." It enacted: "That from and after the 24th day of June, 1750, no mill or other engine for slitting or rolling of iron, or any plating forge to work with a tilt-hammer, or any furnace for making steel, shall be erected, or, after such erection, continued in any of His Majesty's colonies in America; and if any person or persons shall erect, or cause to be erected, or, after such erection, continue, or cause to be continued, in any of the said colonies, any such mill, engine, forge, or furnace, every person or persons so offending shall, for every such mill, engine, forge, or furnace, forfeit the sum of two hundred pounds of lawful money of Great Britain." And further: "That every such mill, engine, forge, or furnace, so erected or continued, contrary to the directions of this act, shall be deemed *a common nuisance*," to be abated by "every governor, lieutenant-governor, or commander-in-chief of any of His Majesty's colonies in America, where any such mill, engine, forge, or furnace shall be erected or continued." This act was enforced down to the beginning of the Revolution.

The Declaration of American Independence recited, among other causes of complaint against the home government, that it had cut off the trade of the colonies "with all parts of the world." How it did this is illustrated in various acts of Parliament which we shall quote.

By the navigation act of 1660 (12 Charles II.) it was provided "that certain specified articles, the produce of the colonies, should not be exported directly from the colonies to any foreign country, but that they should first be sent to Britain and there *unladen* before they could be forwarded to their final destination." Sugar, molasses, tobacco, hides, iron, corn, and lumber were either originally or ultimately embraced within the provisions of this act, the plain intention of which was to give to England a monopoly of the purchase and sale of all colonial products. Robert Ellis Thompson states that "in 1699 the export of wool and woolens from the colonies . . was forbidden. In 1731 an inquiry of the Board of Trade ascertained that the colonies were making linens, woolens, iron wares, paper, hats, and leather, and even exporting hats. The carriage of these, even from one plantation or colony to another, was forbidden."

McCulloch says that, "besides compelling the colonists to *sell* their produce exclusively in the English markets, it was next thought advisable to oblige them to *buy* such foreign articles as they might stand in need of entirely from the merchants and manufacturers of England." For this purpose it was enacted in 1663 that "no commodity of the growth, production, or manufacture of Europe shall be imported into the British plantations but such as are laden and put on board in England, Wales, or Berwick-upon-Tweed, and in English-built shipping, whereof the master and three-fourths of the crew are English."

It will be perceived that the acts of Parliament from which we have quoted were intended to benefit the manufactures of England by destroying those of the colonies, and that they also aimed to secure to her "the absolute monopoly of her colonial commerce." These acts were successful in accomplishing the objects sought, but they formed no insignificant part of that "long train of abuses and usurpations" which led to independence.

In his great work on *The Tariff Question* Erastus B. Bigelow condenses into the following sentences the legislation of Great Britain concerning the introduction into the British Islands of cotton fabrics from India, which once threatened to be a rival of British woolen products: "In 1678 strong remonstrances were made in Parliament against the admission of Indian calicoes, chintzes, and muslins, on the ground that they were ruining the woolen trade. In 1700 an act was passed *prohibiting* the importation of the articles just named, under a penalty, upon the seller and buyer, of £200. In 1720 another concession was made to the demands of the woolen interest. Under the act of this year no person could *wear* a printed calico without the payment of £5 for the privilege, while the seller of the article was mulcted to the extent of £20. Sixteen years later the act of 1720 was so far modified as to legalize the use of *mixed* prints, while the prohibition against using calicoes made wholly of cotton remained in full force. This state of things lasted nearly forty years longer. In 1774 Parliament passed an act sanctioning the manufacture of cotton, and making it lawful to use or *wear* any new fabric made wholly of that material."

An excise duty of "three pence for every yard in length, reckoning yard-wide," was, however, imposed on "the said manufactured stuffs wholly made of cotton spun in Great Britain when printed." This duty, like the act of 1678, requiring that "all dead bodies should be wrapped in woolen shrouds," was for the benefit of the British woolen industry. In a short time the English cotton industry itself demanded and received protection from foreign competition. In his *Letters to the London Times* Henry C. Carey states that the cotton manufacture was transferred from India to Great Britain by prohibiting "the export not only of machinery itself but of all the artisans by whom machines might possibly be made. To this was added the imposition of heavy duties on the import of Indian cottons, coupled with a prohibition of duties of any kind on English cottons imported into India."

The British tariff that was in force in 1787, the year in which the Constitution of the United States was framed, was a very restrictive measure. The word "prohibited" appears in it opposite to many leading productions of other countries, including iron in hoops, rods, cast, and wrought; steel, brass, and copper manufactures; manufactures of silk;

boots and shoes; gloves of leather; leather itself; hats. In the same year paper was subject to a duty of 75 per cent., and cotton manufactures, except from within the limits of the East India Company's charter, to a duty of 44 per cent.

A favorite method of encouraging British manufactures was the payment of government bounties on exports. For instance: In 1819, the importation of silk goods being still prohibited, an act was passed to grant an additional bounty on the exportation of certain silk manufactures of Great Britain. In 1821 another act was passed to grant bounties on the exportation of certain mixed goods of silk and mohair and mohair and worsted, the manufacture of Great Britain. In 1820 an act was passed to continue an act granting a bounty on certain British and Irish linens and reducing duties on imported raw linen yarns. A bounty on the exportation of British wheat was paid from 1689 to 1815.

The nature of the protection which England extended to her iron industry is explained by Dr. Elder as follows: "Iron imported in foreign vessels was charged, as early as the year 1710, with a duty of £2 10s. per ton, which was raised at successive periods, till in 1819 it stood at £6 10s. in English and £7 18s. 6d. in foreign vessels. This was adequate as well as earnest protection of the domestic manufacture, for as early as seven years after the last-mentioned date England was actually producing her own iron at £3 13s. cheaper than the cheapest of her competitors in all Europe. Being thus secure against all rivalry in the home market the duty was reduced in 1834 to £1 per ton."

The iron referred to by Dr. Elder was bar iron. In Scrivenor's *History of the Iron Trade* we find further details of the protective duties which were imposed by Great Britain on foreign iron and steel. "Iron slit, or hammered into rods, and iron drawn down, or hammered, less than three-quarters of an inch square, was made to pay a duty at the rate of £20 per ton; wrought iron, not otherwise enumerated, was taxed with a payment of £50 for every £100 worth imported; and steel, or manufactures of steel, were similarly loaded with a fifty per cent. duty."

A significant feature of the British tariff which was in force in 1819 is found in the large number of articles which were absolutely prohibited from entering British ports, or were subjected to duties of one-half their value. The United States has never prohibited the importation of any useful commodity, except in time of war or in retaliation for the unfriendly action of other countries.

An English writer, Sir Henry Parnell, in his work on *Financial Reform*, gives a summary of a Parliamentary return issued in 1829, from which it appears that, in that year, "protective duties were imposed upon every description of manufacture, of which the following are examples: 30 per cent.—manufactures of brass, copper, lace, leather, silk, embroidery and needle-work, pencils, pens, sealing-wax, hair of goats, wool, pots of stone, varnish; 20 per cent.—japanned ware, wrought iron, manufactures of pewter, steel, and tin jewellery, baskets, boxes, buttons, haberdashery and apparel, scientific and musical instruments, matting, mattresses, cotton and woolen manufactures; 15 per cent.—earthen and china ware, some woolen manufactures, tiles; 40 per cent.—linen manufactures; 50 per cent.—empty casks; 75 per cent.—dressed furs; 25 per cent.—watches; upon many other articles there were specific duties, and upon manufactures not enumerated the rate was 20 per cent.

"In order to protect agriculture the following duties were imposed: Bacon, 28s. per cwt.; butter, 20s. per cwt.; cheese, 10s. 6d. per cwt.; hay, 24s. per load; hops, £8 11s. per cwt.; hemp seed, £2 per quarter; hemp, undressed, 4s. 6d. per cwt.; lard, 8s. per cwt.; mules and asses, 10s. 6d. each; horses, £1 each; rape and linseed oil, £39 18s. per ton; peas, 7s. 6d. per bushel; potatoes, 2s. per cwt.; seeds, £1; tallow, 3s. 2d. per cwt.; tares, 10s. per quarter; timber, £2 15s. per load; wheat, £1 5s. a quarter to 1s., according as the price rose from 61s. to 70s. a quarter; barley, 13s. 10d. to 1s., according as the price rose from 32s. to 40s. a quarter; oats, 10s. 9d. a quarter to 1s., according as the price rose from 24s. to 31s. a quarter; other grain, flour, and meal on similar scales. The importation of living animals for food, and of beef, lamb, mutton, and pork, was *absolutely prohibited*. The lowest rate of duty on sugar was 24s. per cwt., with higher duties upon sugar from other sources than our own colonies; tea was taxed 100 per cent. on its value; and coffee from 6d. to 1s. 3d. per pound, according to the place of its origin."

It was not until 1842 that the British Government seriously began to abandon protective duties, but many years elapsed before their general repeal was effected. Down to 1859 protective duties were still retained on many foreign commodities entering British ports, and in the tariffs of 1851 and 1854 these duties were very prominent. A protective duty on silks, boots and shoes, and gloves continued down to 1860; on timber down to 1866; and on sugar down to 1874. Even in our own day it can scarcely be said that all protective duties have disappeared from the British tariff, for duties on beer and spirits, which benefit English brewers and distillers, are still imposed.

An examination of the British tariffs which have been in force in this century will well reward the reader who has been led to believe that Great Britain has been steadily practicing free trade with all the world from a "time to which the memory of man runneth not to the contrary." Her free trade policy dates only from the early part of Queen Victoria's long reign, but this policy relates only to the withdrawal of protective duties.

The principle of protection for the manufactures of England, Scotland, and Wales is still apparent in the dealings of Great Britain with her present colonies, for her influence is steadily exerted, under various pretexts, as it was with her American colonies in the last century, to prevent them from manufacturing for themselves. It is also apparent in the payment of large annual subsidies to British steamship lines at the present day, which subsidies aid greatly in the extension of British trade with all the world. We may remark further that, in seeking through commercial treaties and other less reputable instrumentalities to prevent other nations from developing their resources, the same principle of protection to her own industries is found to constitute the cornerstone of all the diplomacy of the British nation.

# CHAPTER III.

### THE BRITISH WORKINGMAN UNDER VICTORIA AND HER IMMEDIATE PREDECESSORS.

The celebration in June, 1897, of the conclusion of sixty years of Queen Victoria's reign has called forth many comments upon the causes of the prosperity which has been so prominent a feature of this remarkable period in English history. Undoubtedly the leading cause of this prosperity is to be found in the extraordinary extension of British trade.

A writer in *The Forum* for July, 1897, Professor Thomas Davidson, who was born a British subject, says that, coincidently with the accession of Victoria to the throne in 1837, there "was an outburst of productive and commercial enterprise and an extension of the field of commerce such as had never before been witnessed. The British were soon the first industrial and trading people of the world." Professor Davidson does not say that this industrial pre-eminence had been secured by the steady, persistent, cruel, and remorseless warfare of British manufacturers, aided by British diplomacy, for the control of foreign markets, but he comes very near to telling the whole truth in the following sentences: "It has been mainly through the efforts of British merchants to *extend their markets* that the British nation in the last sixty years has come to *extend its territory. Markets those merchants were determined to have everywhere.* Among people ready for them they at once established them: *peoples not ready they undertook to make ready or else to replace.*"

Not satisfied with the control of their own markets British manufacturers have sought to supply the world's markets by means which a British Parliamentary commission described in 1854 as follows: "The laboring classes generally in the manufacturing districts of this country, and especially in the iron and coal districts, are very little aware of the extent to which they are often indebted for their being employed at all to the immense losses which their employers voluntarily incur in bad times in order *to destroy foreign competition and to gain and keep possession of foreign markets. . . The large capitals of this country are the great instruments of warfare against the competing capital of foreign countries.*" The Chinese opium war in the early part of the reign of Queen Victoria, which compelled the Chinese to legalize the trade in British opium, was something else than a war of capital. It was real and bloody *war*. No other nation of modern times —neither Germany, nor France, nor the United States, has sought to *force* its manufactured products upon other countries or to prevent those countries from manufacturing for themselves.

The writer in *The Forum* does not consider the effect upon her own people of the industrial warfare which Great Britain has waged against other nations, at first with the aid of the most stringent protective tariff legislation the world has ever known and afterwards through a free trade policy dating from 1846. Has this warfare resulted in elevating the men whose sweat has most promoted it? We know that through it the ruling classes of Great Britain have prospered, but how have *the masses* been fed and clothed, and in what kind of homes have *they* lived and died? What have been *their* opportunities for rising in the world, or even for the enjoyment of an old age of peace and comfort? The policy of Great Britain which has sought to crush the manufactures of other nations has not produced the highest moral, social, and intellectual development of which her working people are capable. Great Britain has subordinated the best interests of her toiling masses and the highest capabilities of the nation to her unworthy greed of present gain. The proofs of this assertion are only too abundant, and they are mainly furnished by British witnesses.

The London *Fortnightly Review* stated in 1875 that "for more than four hundred years" after the dawn of civilization in Europe, namely, from the fourteenth century down to the beginning of the nineteenth century, it was the "*settled policy*" of British legislators that it was "*a crime* for a workman to seek higher wages. . . So late as 1720 an act was passed to keep down the wages of the tailors of London and Westminster. Any master who gave more than was allowed by the act was liable to a fine of £5; every workman who asked more was to be imprisoned for two months." Down to 1799 restrictions upon the liberty of "the masters" to raise wages voluntarily were retained in British laws, and down to 1824 it was a punishable offense at common law as well as by statute in England and Scotland for mechanics to form societies for the purpose of peacefully endeavoring to raise their wages. In 1762 the court at Edinburgh found "that the defenders and other journeymen tailors of Edinburgh are not entitled to an hour of recess for breakfast, that the wages of a journeyman tailor in the said city ought not to exceed one shilling per day, and that if any journeyman tailor not retained or employed shall refuse to work when requested by a master on the aforesaid terms, unless for some sufficient cause to be allowed by the magistrates, the offender shall, upon conviction, be punished in terms of law." It was not until 1871 that trade-unions were legalized in Great Britain. It must be remembered that these organizations owe their origin to the oppression of labor, and that, but for them, the British workingman would to-day be more of a slave and less of a freeman than he is.

Other facts may be cited to prove that it has always been the spirit of the British laws to hedge about with difficulties the efforts of the British laborer to better his condition. In the fourteenth century, when agriculture was regarded with more favor than manufactures, legislation was employed to prevent the sons of agricultural laborers from learning trades. We have shown that laws prohibiting skilled workmen from going abroad were rigidly enforced in the eighteenth century and in the early part of the nineteenth century.

The following remarkable statement we take from a paper upon the industries of Scotland, contained in the Report of the Secretary of State of the United States for 1868 upon our Foreign Relations. "The lot of the early miners and coal-bearers in Scotland was rendered hard enough by their having to work in the face of many dangers and difficulties, to the removal of which science had not then been applied, but their condition was made more wretched by a system of bondage or serfdom. On entering a coal mine the workers became bound to labor therein during their whole lifetime; and in the case of sale or alienation of the ground on which a colliery was situated the right to their services passed to the purchaser without any special grant or agreement. The sons of the collier could not follow any occupation save that of their father, and could labor only in the mine to which they were held to be attached by birth. Tramps and vagabonds, who were not sufficiently wicked to deserve hanging, and on whom prison accommodations would only be wasted, were sometimes consigned by the lords of justiciary to lifelong service in the collieries and salteries. Every man thus disposed of *had riveted on his neck a collar*, on which was engraved the name of the person to whom he was gifted, together with the date. The collar was intended as a check upon deserters; and constables were highly rewarded when they brought back a fugitive. A collar of the kind referred to may be seen in the Edinburgh Antiquarian Museum. Though serfdom had a considerable time previously died out, so far as all other classes of workers were concerned, colliers and salters were not liberated until towards the close of the last century; and the custom of celebrating the anniversary of their emancipation has not yet died out. The act which set them free was passed on the 23d of May, 1775."

In his *Work and Wages* Mr. Thomas Brassey, a loyal Englishman, remarks: "So long as the cost of production in this country exceeds the cost of production in other countries the neutral markets of the world will no longer draw their supplies from England. The demand for labor here will accordingly diminish; the multitudes of people out of employ will be *driven*, under the pressure of *necessity*, to compete against each other for employment; *wages will then be in proportion diminished* until we are once more in a position to compete." Mr. Brassey also says: "It is solely by our *lower prices* that we have secured the *monopoly* of the Syrian market." Labor being the principal element in the cost of most of the commodities which Great Britain sells abroad the plain inference from these extracts is that British workingmen must be systematically underpaid and degraded that the condition of *cheapness* may be secured.

In a speech in Parliament on the budget in 1866 Mr. Gladstone declared that "during the last twenty-five years" British commerce "had trebled, mainly in consequence of our mineral treasures. It was important to bear in mind that it was not the quantity of our coal but its production *at a low price* that had given us the start." In an address before the Social Science Congress at Liverpool in 1876 Mr. Shaw-Lefevre said: " With cheap coal, with abundant capital, *with reduced wages*, I see no reason to fear for the future, and no grave apprehension for foreign competition."

In its issue for the 25th of March, 1876, Ryland's *Iron Trade Circular*, published at Birmingham, stated that the British people were "gradually coming to a more reasonable range of prices, through concessions which have been *wrung* from ironworkers and colliers." That one word "wrung" gives the key to the whole labor problem of Great Britain. The same paper on the 6th of May of the same year, alluding to labor troubles in the British iron trade, told its readers that "the result will be either no work at all or *submit to the inevitable.*"

In his *Sophisms of Free Trade*, first printed in 1849, Sir John Barnard Byles, an eminent Englishman, thus states the inevitable tendency of all efforts to undersell other nations in their own markets: "In the fierce struggle of *universal competition those whom the climate enables or misery forces or slavery compels to live worst and produce cheapest will necessarily beat out of the market and starve those whose wages are better.* It is a struggle between the working classes of all nations which shall descend first and nearest to the condition of the *brutes.*" The challenge to all the world to produce the cheapest goods may also cause a terrible struggle to preserve even the home market. The Spitalfields silk weaver told Mr. Mayhew: " We've driven the French out of the market in umbrellas and parasols, *but the people are starving while they're driving of 'em out.*"

Joseph Kay, an authorized representative of the University of Cambridge, England, deals exhaustively with the sad condition of British workingmen in a work published in London in 1850, entitled *Social Condition of the People of England and Europe.* In this work he says: "The poor of England are more depressed, more pauperized, more numerous in comparison to the other classes, more irreligious, and very much worse educated than the poor of any other European nation, solely excepting Russia, Turkey, South Italy, Portugal, and Spain. . . In England and Wales more than half the poor can not read and write, while the majority of the remainder know . . very little of the Scripture history. . . Throughout the greater part of Western Europe and North America there is free trade in land, and the peasants can always, by exercising industry, self-denial, and prudence, make themselves proprietors; in England and Wales it is impossible for a peasant to purchase a piece of land." Queen Victoria had been thirteen years on the throne when Mr. Kay's book appeared.

Judge Byles confirms what Mr. Kay says of the inability of the poor man in England and Wales to obtain a piece of land. "Yeomen living on their own small properties were formerly the principal cultivators in England and Wales. With no outgoing for rent, and none for wages, . . the well-grown, robust, and ruddy English yeoman was the most independent of mankind. Such was the English subject of Charles the First. . . Unhappily the race is now almost extinct: large estates and large farms have absorbed them." The yeomen described by the learned judge have become "almost extinct" because the British Government has long maintained a system of land tenure which could have no other result than to enable the rich lord to crush out the small land owner.

Mr. Kay says: "The word *cottage* has ceased to mean what it once meant—a small house surrounded by its little plot of ground, which the inmate might cultivate as he pleased, for the support and gratification of his family and himself." It has *never* been the policy of the British Government to assist its poorer subjects to obtain homes for themselves. It now favors free trade in foreign products which compete with the labor of these poorer subjects, but free trade in land has ceased to be even a dream: as the British Government is now constituted it is an impossibility. In 1844 the London *Times* declared that "*once a peasant in England and the man must remain a peasant forever.*"

The *Modern Doomsday Book* showed a quarter of a century ago that 12,000 persons own thirty of the thirty-seven million acres of land in England and Wales. About twenty persons own the half of all Scotland. Seventeen persons in England and Wales own more than 50,000 acres each, and three of these own over 100,000 acres each. Seven hundred and twenty-nine Englishmen are said by another authority to own half the land in Ireland.

A writer in *Harper's Magazine* for August, 1874, remarks that "the most obtrusive fact in the English social system is the contrast which exists between the enormous wealth of the few and the desperate and hopeless poverty of the many." Lord Napier bore similar testimony in an address delivered scarcely a generation ago in London. "The proportion of those who possess to those who possess nothing is probably smaller in some parts of England at this moment than it ever was in any settled community, except in some of the republics of antiquity, where the business of mechanical industry was delegated to slaves."

In the London *Contemporary Review* for March, 1876, the Duke of Argyll says: "As regards the number of those who live by the possession of small agricultural properties it is probably true that the number *rather tends to diminish than to increase*." In the London *Fortnightly Review* for January, 1876, Mr. F. Barham Zincke says: "There are many parishes in which not a man resident in the parish owns a rood of land in it or even the house in which he lives. . . Everybody notices the poverty and meanness of social life in our country towns. . . We can have no good general markets in our towns, large as they are, because the peasant proprietors of the neighborhood have been *extinguished*. To find these natural producers of vegetables, fruit, poultry, eggs, and butter we must now go *beyond the sea*."

If *land* were free in England, Scotland, Wales, and Ireland, so that a part of the population that is now dependent upon mills and factories could be supported by the soil which the aristocracy withholds from cultivation because it is required for their pleasure, and if British manufacturers did not greedily aim to undersell other nations in their own markets, but were content to supply them only with those products which they do not themselves manufacture, it would not be necessary to beat down the wages of the British workingman. It is because the British workingman is *compelled* to become a factory or a mill hand, or a collier, *in competition with all the world*, that he is so hardly dealt with. If the way were open for him to become a small farmer, or if the owner of the factory or mill or colliery were not led to reduce wages to the lowest possible limit of human endurance that he might control foreign markets, the condition of the British workingman would be one which all the world might envy, and England would be "Merrie England" in reality to all her people.

The vital principle of all trade monopoly is the subjugation of labor. Education, religion, the comforts of home, humanity itself, it does not recognize. These are matters of sentiment only to the manufacturer who is wholly intent on seizing his neighbor's trade, and sentiment is not business. Mr. Huskisson told the British House of Commons, in his speech on the 28th of April, 1825 : "If capital had not a fair remuneration here it would seek for it in America. To give it a fair remuneration *the price of labor must be kept down.*" The acts of the British Parliament for the protection of children and for shortening the hours of labor met with very great opposition from the masters. The British workingman drinks because British statesmen and manufacturers offer to him the public house as something better than his cheerless home. The latter do not as a rule pay him sufficient wages to enable him to rent, much less to buy, a comfortable house. They never have done this except when, through the operation of trade-unions or because of a sudden demand for manufactured products, they could not help themselves.

Professor Huxley, the British scientist, once wrote : "A population whose labor is insufficiently remunerated must become physically and morally unhealthy and socially unstable, and, though it may succeed for awhile in industrial competition by reason of the cheapness of its produce, it must in the end fall through hideous misery and degradation to utter ruin."

John Bright once declared that there are one million persons who are paupers on the parish in England, and that "another million are perpetually lingering on the very verge of pauperism." Sir S. Morton Peto, in his treatise on *Taxation*, published in 1863, page 242, says: "It is an awful consideration that in England, abounding as it does with wealth and prosperity, there are nearly a *million* of human beings receiving indoor and outdoor relief as paupers in the different unions, besides the still greater number dependent upon the hand of charity. As the population of England and Wales, by the last census, was 20,205,504 it follows that nearly one-twentieth part of our people are subsisting upon charity!" Other and later authorities place the number of actual paupers in Great Britain at much higher figures.

That British workingmen are capable of the highest intellectual, moral, and social development is shown in the career of a large majority of those Englishmen, Scotchmen, Welshmen, and Irishmen who have escaped from the shores of their native country to become citizens of Australia, New Zealand, Van Diemen's Land, South Africa, Canada, and the United States.

# CHAPTER IV.

### THE HOPELESS POOR OF GREAT BRITAIN.

UNLIKE the England of song and story the England of Queen Victoria's time is not merry with the daily life of a contented and comfortable and well-paid working people. Numerous English authorities of undoubted credit may be quoted to prove this fact.

Mr. John Noble, an English economic writer, testifies as follows: "In 1848 the great bulk of the people had ceased to know anything of butcher's meat except as an occasional Sunday luxury." Professor J. E. Thorold Rogers, an eminent English writer, said about 1870 that "the cost of living in country districts has doubled within the last thirty years," and that "some articles of food, once within the reach of all, are now practically unattainable by country people." In 1869 Sir Edward Sullivan, of Lancashire, England, declared that the operatives in the manufacturing districts were not prosperous. "It is a mockery to tell them to thank God for a full stomach when they are empty! They are *not* well off; never has starvation, pauperism, crime, discontent, been so plentiful in the manufacturing districts."

Concerning the condition of the laboring classes of Scotland an extract from the report of the city chamberlain of Glasgow for 1869 is suggestive of far more than is said. "By the census of 1861 more than 28,000 houses in Glasgow were found to consist of but a single apartment each, and above 32,000 of but two, so that, of the whole 82,000 families comprising the city, upward of 60,000 were housed in dwellings of one and two apartments each." Edward Young, an officer of the United States Government, visited Scotland in 1869, and upon his return he wrote and published in the New York *Independent* the following: "Having been taught to believe that in respect to education and morals the people of Scotland were far in advance of those of most other countries it was with profound disappointment and heartfelt regret that I witnessed the painful evidences of ignorance and intemperance among the working classes of Glasgow."

There is a class of working people in Great Britain who should above all others be well fed and comfortably housed, for there is no good reason why they should not be, namely, the agricultural laborers. But they are miserably poor. A Parliamentary commission about the close of the third quarter of the nineteenth century, appointed to inquire into the condition of the agricultural laborers, reported that "in Dorsetshire vegetables flavored with bacon fat, or bread and cheese; in Somersetshire brown bread dipped in cider; in Cheshire potatoes, or gruel thickened with treacle, are the commonest articles of food." An American, writing from London in 1875, says: "To the modern British rustic plenty of any kind is unknown for at least four-fifths of the year. At harvest-time, perhaps, he can eat and drink his fill, but for the rest of the year his life is spent in a daily fight against the grim giant of starvation. His food consists of bread without butter, potatoes, milk, bacon once or twice a week, and at rare intervals a piece of beef or mutton, and these only in quantities barely sufficient to sustain life. In the winter time, when work is scarce, even this meagre supply fails, and he is compelled to fall back upon the parish for assistance." The London *Times* for October 27, 1874, more than confirms the truthfulness of this picture.

Judge Byles says: "*The furies of want, misery, and despair scourge the emigrants from our shores.*" A writer in *Fraser's Magazine* (London) for January, 1848, says: "*The worst horrors of the slave-trade have been enacted in the flight of British subjects from their native shores.*"

Ireland's pitiful condition during the reign of Queen Victoria is shown in the statistics of Irish population. In 1841 the population of Ireland was 8,199,853. In 1891 it was 4,704,750. Famine, emigration, and free trade have reduced the population of Ireland in fifty years of Queen Victoria's reign over 42 per cent.

In Great Britain it is a common sight to see women and children engaged in employments to which they are wholly unsuited. In the London *Iron* for May 29, 1875, we read the following: "The public have been frequently horrified by tales of the oppression and demoralization of young women in the nail-making districts, and now, thanks to the Chainmakers' Association, like revelations have been made, in connection with another branch of ironwork, of an evil which has been going on for a considerable period unnoticed until the local press brought it under the eye of the public. Visiting Cradley Heath, in company with a deputation of the above-named association, the special commissioner of the Wolverhampton *Daily News* entered a smithy where he found 'a graceful, fair-haired girl of fifteen summers' turning out links of twisted dog-chain. The work, especially in summer, is laborious and continuous—'there is no break, no intermission for a single moment. From the anvil to the bellows, and back again, it goes on from morning to night, day after day.' And the days are of eleven or twelve hours each, if not longer. The poor girl thus interviewed scarcely knew, indeed, how long she worked; but she had eighteen chains to make before she finished that day. Neither had she any idea how much she earned, for her mother took the money. There is even worse than this behind. In the summer time we are told the temperature is such that both men and women strip to the waist. Many of these women are married, and the husbands of many of them are living in comparative idleness on the labor of their universally overworked wives. The commission and deputation visited an immense number of shops in Cradley and neighboring villages, and found in all of them girls and women of all ages working in the same unwomanly way. . . From what could be gathered some of the poor creatures toil unceasingly at the forge twelve or thirteen hours a day for from 6s. to 7s. a week."

In the London *Times* of Tuesday, September 28, 1875, is published a statement from Mr. Baker, inspector of factories, for the half year ending with April, 1875, which gives extracts from a remarkable report made to him by Mr. Sub-Inspector Brewer on the nail and chain district of the Black Country, from which we quote: "I am continually asked whether I can not do something to stop women's labor, especially in and around Hulesowen, (where hundreds work, making the large nails or spikes,) and where it is the order of the day, and is far fitter for men than for women. And these women work night and day, and toil and slave, and for what? Not for the price that straightforward masters would give, but for any price any crafty knave of a master chooses to offer. Day by day I am more and more convinced that this women's labor is the bane of this place. Nor do I confine this remark to the nail and chain trade alone. . . Nor is this state of things confined to the Black Country."

In 1892 Nathaniel McKay, of New York, visited England and upon his return he testified as follows: "I saw thousands of women working for 1 shilling 3 pence a day, making chains from 7 o'clock in the morning until 9 o'clock at night." About the time of Mr. McKay's visit John Burnett, a labor commissioner, made an investigation of the condition of the nail and chain makers of South Staffordshire and East Worcestershire, and reported as follows: "T. Fasback, whose shop I visited, seemed a steady, respectable man. In a good week he said he could clear 12 shillings. His boy there, who was over fourteen years old, could earn 3 shillings 6 pence by working from 7 to 7. He had also a daughter of twenty-three, who made traces and could earn 5 shillings 6 pence, and a girl of seventeen, who could earn 3 shillings 6 pence. A question as to how much it cost them for butcher's meat was received with scornful laughter. Meat and potatoes, it appeared, was a treat reserved for Sundays only, and very often they did not have any then."

The London *Iron*, referring to this subject, said that Lord Shaftesbury (a second Howard) had "taken up the cause of the unfortunate women whose sad condition Mr. Inspector Baker's report has made public." The same paper for July 10, 1875, referred in the following language to the condition of the factory operatives in Manchester: "Previous to the successful termination of the movement for the emancipation of what were by no extravagant figure of speech denominated 'white slaves,' whose emancipation was as strenuously opposed by their masters as that of the negroes was by theirs, one of the most painful spectacles to be witnessed in Manchester or any of the cotton towns was that presented by the issuing from one of the large factories of its crowd of pale-faced, stunted, and crippled operatives."

The London *Mining Journal* for October 10, 1885, says: "The employment of girls and women at coal mines has long been a standing reproach to some of our mine owners. The total number of females employed at coal mines in 1884 was 4,458, of which 329 were between the ages of 13 and 16 and 3 between 10 and 13. In 1883, however, the total number employed was 4,479, of which one was between 10 and 13 and 288 between 13 and 16, so that there was a decrease of 21 in 1884 as compared with the previous year. The late Lord Shaftesbury succeeded in forcing females out of the mines in Great Britain, and the time has certainly come, in our opinion, when they should not be allowed to work on the pit banks. *The only reason that can be assigned for their employment is that they do a certain amount of work for less money than it would be done for by men.*" The report of Her Majesty's inspectors of mines for 1896 shows that 5,114 women and girls were employed in that year at British coal and other mines. In England thousands of young girls are still employed in carrying clay in the brickyards.

In the evidence taken at Wolverhampton in 1875, before the Royal Commissioner appointed to inquire into the working of the Workshop and Factory Acts, the following facts were elicited: That boys under ten years are permitted to work in the coal-pits, and boys under twelve years to work full time and all night in the iron trade; that large numbers of young girls and young boys not attending school work regularly in the brickyards; that the employment of women on the pit-banks is their "common industry" in Shropshire and Wigan, and that their work is "very hard—worse than nail and chain making;" and that if women were prevented from working at the collieries and in similar employments "*it would have the effect of making ironstone 7s. per ton more than now, because large wages would have to be given to the men to do the work.*" Mr. John Sparrow, of the Bilston iron works and Millfields furnaces, stated to the Commissioner that his business was seriously interrupted because he was prohibited from employing boys under thirteen years as *underhand puddlers*. At the first regular meeting of the British Iron Trade Association, held at London in February, 1876, Mr. Bleckley, of Warrington, a member, remarked that "*he considered it a hardship that children of twelve years of age were not allowed to work in the rolling mills.*" The London *Iron and Coal Trades Review* for May 3, 1895, contains a long report of an interview on May 1st of a deputation of the British Iron Trade Association with the Home Secretary of Her Majesty's Government, in which the ironmasters vigorously protested against that feature of the new Factories and Workshops bill, then pending in the House of Commons, which proposed to extend the age at which boys may be employed *at night* from 14 to 16 years.

At the Woolen Trade Banquet in New York, on December 14, 1870, the Hon. William E. Dodge, president of the Chamber of Commerce of the City of New York, delivered an address, in which he said: "The term, now so generally used, of 'pauper labor,' which our free trade papers use in such derision, has yet in it a great deal of truth. I have visited many of the large manufactories of England and have seen evidences of poverty which I trust our laborers will never experience. I have seen in the iron mills of Wales young girls, with their heavy shoes and short woolen dresses, wheeling iron, cinder, coals, etc., at night, among the half-naked puddlers, doing the work done by men and boys in our mills, and receiving for a week's wages what we pay for a day."

How cheaply female labor in Wales may *now* be obtained can easily be inferred from the frank admission of the London *Iron and Steel Trades Journal* for April 12, 1890. That paper then said: "*The great obstacle to tinplate making on a large scale in the States is the entire absence of cheap female labor, so necessary in the industry and so abundant in Wales.*" The same paper for December 5, 1891, is even more candid. It tells its readers that "in Wales the adult workpeople have been engaged in the tinplate trade from childhood, and their children, as soon as capable, assist in the mills. It is, indeed, not an uncommon occurrence to find whole families working together. The making of tinplates as the children grow to men and women becomes a habit, and they acquire great dexterity, saving much time and labor, and *the wages of the female laborers and children are but a tithe of what American skilled workmen would demand.*"

Less than a score of years before Mr. Dodge's experience it was lawful in Great Britain for children as young as seven years to work in cotton factories and at other employments, and thousands of these innocents were thus employed.

A few years prior to Victoria's accession the pitiful condition of the children employed in English factories became a subject of public comment, and apparently for the first time. In John Ashton's *When William IV. Was King*, printed by D. Appleton & Co. in 1897, we read what one Tory champion of the helpless factory children said in 1832 in a speech at Huddersfield: "Take then a little captive, and I will not picture fiction to you, but I will tell you what I have seen. Take a little captive six years old; she shall rise from her bed at 4 o'clock in the morning of a cold winter's day; but before that she wakes perhaps half a dozen times and says, 'Father, is it time? Father, is it time?' And at last, when she gets up, and puts her little bits of rags upon her weary limbs, weary with the last day's work, she trudges onward through rain and snow to the mill, perhaps two miles, or at least one mile; and there, for thirteen, fourteen, fifteen, sixteen, seventeen, or even eighteen hours, she is obliged to work, with only thirty minutes' interval. The girl I am speaking of died, but she dragged on that dreadful existence for several years. Homeward again at night she would go, when she was able; but many a time she hid herself in the wool at the mill, as she had not strength to go. But this is not an isolated case. I wish it were." Nothing of consequence was done for nearly twenty years to mitigate the evils complained of by this Tory speaker.

Rev. Benjamin Waugh, who appears to be an English clergyman, pictures as follows in May, 1897, the condition of the children of England's poor at the accession of Victoria to the British throne in 1837: "The sight of its activities under the earth, in coal and metallic mines, would suggest a land as intelligently benighted, as destitute even of a single star of justice, for, at least, the children found there, as the mines themselves are of the light of the sun. Let the imaginary traveler leave the damp, dark mines, and enter the factories picturesquely situated by wooded streams, sights pitiable as those we associate with the cotton plantations of slavery would deepen the impression received from the world underground. Turning to the bricks of which the factories were built the traveler would find them stained with the tears, almost tears of blood, of little lives which had toiled and sickened in making them out of the clay of the fields from which they had been brought. He would see in the fields of agriculture gangs of child stone-pickers, and stooping toilers he would see in all weathers wearing out their young lives under the 'gangers'' orders, and on the canal boatloads of little paupers going to the Children's Market. Guardians literally sold their children to any one who would buy them. As small human lives capable of suffering and of happiness they had no value ; *their value was to enable trade to produce, and to supply markets with a cheap abundance.* In homes where nature had its way and the family was true to family instincts children were, of course, looked upon as they are to-day; but to the children of the dead poor, and the children of the worthless living, children unloved and unwanted, to be counted by tens of thousands, treated worse than infant slaves were treated, the attitude of Parliament, which ought to have been one of interest, was one of indifference."

These wrongs to children have been largely righted during the reign of Queen Victoria, but not wholly. That they should have had an existence at so late a period in the world's history as the beginning and early part of her reign, and in England of all other European countries, is a shameful fact, to say the least.

Mr. Kay's book is filled with evidence showing that drunkenness, immorality, brutality, Sabbath-breaking, poaching, rank ignorance, small and crowded tenements, insufficient food, diseases incident to lack of proper nourishment, and excessively filthy habits and surroundings are characteristics of large numbers of the working classes of England, Scotland, and Wales. The reader of Mr. Kay's book passes over the narrative of these conditions with a shudder. The responsibility for the low condition of morality and the miserable character of the habitations among the working classes of England and Wales is ascribed by Mr. Kay to "the low rate of wages" they receive, to the neglect of their intellectual and moral training by the authorities, to the utter indifference of the masters to their comfort, and to the lack in every breast of a cheerful hope of better days. Mr. Kay states that in Byrnmaur "nearly every family is in the employment of Mr. Bailey, the ironmaster, whose works are at Nantyglo. The town reeks with dirt; there are no lamps or effective drainage; and . . not the slightest step has been taken to improve the mental or moral condition of the violent and vicious community. Neither church nor school has been established by those who employ the people or own the land; and the only step that has been taken for their benefit is that of establishing within a week or two of this time a police station." These words were printed in 1850.

In Benjamin Disraeli's *Sybil*, first printed in 1845, there are to be found appalling pictures of wretchedness and misery among the working men and women and the children of England that we have no heart to reproduce even in the faintest outline. That these pictures were copied from real life and were not works of the imagination the distinguished author certifies in the "advertisement" which forms the introduction to his remarkable book. When it was first printed Queen Victoria had been on the throne eight years. Walter Besant and other recent English writers have given accounts of English wretchedness and misery that are fully as truthful and graphic as the story of *Sybil.* Mrs. Annie Besant and even John Ruskin have narrated harrowing tales of the painful and frequently unsuccessful efforts of the poor of London to keep themselves from starving.

Of the needlewomen of London at the present day Mrs. Besant says: "Our death rate is heavy there. They die of starvation, of low fever, of bronchitis, of all diseases that feed on underclothed and underfed bodies. Women work thirteen, fourteen, fifteen hours, with nothing to make them strong or warm but the hot water they call tea and a thin shawl that has seen many winters. The cold strikes home, and they say at the hospital, 'bronchitis.' It is not. It is slow starvation. We kill women by the thousand, while their sisters go diamond-decked. That is London in its wealth and its poverty."

In a report of the Christian Instruction Society of Great Britain which appeared in 1897 one of its agents says: "Two widows I know of in Mile-End, New Town, who make sunshades and umbrellas. For one dozen of the former, and using her own thread, and making them entirely, the maker gets six pence; for the latter 1 shilling a dozen. They take in their work every evening, sit up late, and rise early, with little nourishment, if any, to get the work done." These are literally starvation wages. The case is one of thousands.

Of the struggle for existence of the dock laborers of London Mrs. Besant says: "You must get up early or stay up late in order to see the struggle here. You must be at the dock gates by 2 or 3 o'clock in the morning. There are 20,000 to 25,000 men gathered around the gates, for the earliest there get the first chance. A man appears and calls out for so many. Then begins a literal fight for life. Arms and ribs have been broken in the struggle. Surgeons say that more than sixty per cent. of these men are injured by accidents. The work needs strength, and many are faint from hunger. They often fall into the water on account of imperfect appliances, and are struck by the swinging bales. One-third are always turned away without employment, to go back to hungry wives and children crying for lack of food."

General William Booth, of the Salvation Army, in his book entitled *In Darkest England*, printed in 1890, after Queen Victoria had been on the throne fifty-three years, describes the destitution and the degradation of the poor of London in language which is sickening. The facts which he narrates in convincing detail would be a reproach to the most barbarous race of men and women that the world has ever known. To his terrible picture of destitution among the working classes of London and other parts of England he adds the opinion that "deaths from actual hunger are more common than is generally supposed."

The Rev. Stopford Brooke says: "We are pre-eminent in London in these matters. There is nothing so terrible in any other civilized city—no, not even in Paris or New York. *There is nowhere else in the Christian world such a mass of wretchedness, squalor, and degradation as in England.*"

The brutality which is so prominent a feature of the social life of large numbers of colliers and other British laborers is the product in large part of the influences already stated—low wages, no prospect of ever owning a home of any kind, a lack of common-school education, and a lack of suitable religious training. Not even among the North American Indians do we find examples of greater brutality than are narrated in the columns of English newspapers.

Dogs in the mining districts of England are frequently treated with far more tenderness and consideration than the children of the pitmen.

It is sometimes alleged as an apology for the destitution and wretchedness so generally found in Great Britain that leading cities in the United States are themselves great social ulcers—nurseries of pauperism and vice. This statement is true, but the fact should not be forgotten that a large proportion of the paupers and criminals found in our large cities are *foreigners*, who are in no sense a product of our industrial policy or political institutions. They belong to a class of immigrants who are not welcome here and are largely incapable of reformation and improvement. If it were possible to prevent them from coming to our country the destitution and crime which now prevail in American cities would be largely reduced, and all Europe, Great Britain included, would have more paupers and more criminals than it now has, and all its own.

In a speech at Rochdale, in December, 1879, John Bright said that "the American tariff must be held to be *very barbarous*." If any treatment of workingmen and their families and of the helpless poor can be found to be more "barbarous" than that which has been habitually meted out to these classes in Great Britain during the reign of Queen Victoria and under a free trade policy, and which has been only imperfectly described in the preceding pages, Mr. Bright has not indicated where the proofs of this treatment are to be found.

## CHAPTER V.

### THE BRITISH POLICY OF FREE TRADE.

It is claimed by Mr. Gladstone and other Englishmen that the prosperity of Great Britain during Queen Victoria's reign has been due to the British policy of free trade which was established in 1846, and that, under this policy, the wages of British workingmen have been increased. But the Sheffield *Telegraph* assured Mr. Gladstone in 1891 that the improved condition of British labor "is no more to be attributed to free imports, miscalled free trade, than the existence of the Goodwin Sands is to be credited to the neighborhood of the steeple of Tenterden Church," and in the same year the London *Times*, also replying to Mr. Gladstone, said: "Workingmen, however, know that a corresponding improvement has been the rule in countries where protection has been enforced most stringently, in France and Germany, and still more remarkably in the United States."

The *Telegraph* discusses this subject further as follows: "To what causes is the increase of British wages since 1860 assignable? First, to protection. The remarkable development of manufactures in the United States during the decade 1860–70, together with the paucity of American labor during its first five years, which were years of war, created a rate of compensation for labor which up to that time would have been regarded as fabulous. *British manufacturers had to raise the pay of their workmen or see the best of them leave in mass for the United States.* The large outputs of gold and silver in America, Africa, and Australia also may have had something to do with increasing British wages by increasing the volume of money in circulation. *But the wonderful increase of American wages and industries between 1860 and 1870 probably was the starting point of the British increase."*

The improvement in the wages of British workingmen during Queen Victoria's reign, as has already been shown, has not been shared by millions of the poor of Great Britain, so that, even if Mr. Gladstone's claim were true, there must be something radically wrong in a system of political economy which stimulates only special industries and does not in any way aim to lift up the helpless masses.

In a speech at Toledo, Ohio, on February 12, 1891, William McKinley, then a Representative in Congress, quoted Charles Kingsley, "whose memory is cherished wherever the English tongue is spoken," as follows: "Next you have the Manchester school, from which Heaven defend us! For all narrow, conceited, hypocritical, and anarchic schemes of the universe the Cobden and Bright one is exactly the worst. To pretend to be the workman's friends by keeping down the price of bread when all they want thereby *is to keep down wages and increase profits, and in the meantime to widen the gulf between the workingman and all that is time-honored and chivalrous in English society*, that they may make the men their divided slaves—that is, perhaps half unconsciously, for there are excellent men among them, the game of the Manchester school."

The Manchester school to which Charles Kingsley referred is the school of free trade. That it has unduly and abnormally, even if successfully, built up the manufacturing industries of Great Britain should be conceded; that it has done this by sacrificing the comfort and welfare of millions of the skilled and unskilled working people of Great Britain free trade writers should frankly confess.

In the same speech Mr. McKinley quoted as follows the words of Cardinal Manning, written in December, 1890, and published in the *Nineteenth Century*, an English magazine. Speaking of free trade, "freedom of trade," the Cardinal said: "This freedom of trade has immensely multiplied all branches of commerce and developed the energies of all our industrial population. But it has created two things—the irresponsible wealth, which stagnates, *and the starvation wages of the labor market.* In four of our western counties wages are so low that men come to London by thousands every year, and, being here, crowd the dock-gates and underbid the permanent workingmen, who have already reason not to be content with their hire. We have these two worlds always and openly face to face—the world of wealth and the world of want; the world of wealth saying in its heart, 'I sit as queen over all toilers and traders,' and the world of want not knowing what may be on the morrow. Every city and town has its unemployed. Millions are in poverty."

When Richard Cobden was engaged more than fifty years ago in denouncing the protective policy which was then in force in Great Britain he said in one of his speeches: "When I go down to the manufacturing districts I know that I shall be returning to a gloomy scene. I know that *starvation is stalking through the land, and that men are perishing for want of the merest necessaries of life.*" Mr. Cobden, Mr. Bright, and others succeeded in substituting the British policy of free trade for the British policy of protection, but the testimony of Charles Kingsley, Cardinal Manning, and other authorities we have quoted proves that under free trade the starvation that Mr. Cobden referred to is still "stalking through the land," and that in "Merrie England" men and women and children are still "perishing for want of the merest necessaries of life." Whether under protection or under free trade the steady, persistent, and uncompromising aim of the manufacturing and commercial classes of Great Britain has always been to advance their own interests regardless of the weal or wo of the poor people who must work for such wages as are given to them or starve.

Nor have the agricultural interests of Great Britain prospered under the teachings of the Manchester school. They have fared as badly under the free trade of Queen Victoria's reign as they did hundreds of years ago before a protective tariff first formed a part of the economic policy of the English Government. English agriculture languished, as did all other English industries, until the predecessors of Queen Victoria began the work of protecting English industries against foreign competition; it is again languishing because of the withdrawal of protection fifty years ago. We quote as follows from an article in the New York *Sun* for August 24, 1897.

"Official and conclusive proof of the irreparable decline of farming in Great Britain is furnished in the lately published report of the Royal Commission on agricultural depression. The commission was appointed in 1893; it has sat 177 days; it has heard many scores of voluntary witnesses, and it has profited by the expert observations of agents delegated to visit specially selected areas in England, Wales, and Scotland. The gross annual value of land in England and Wales, which in 1879–80 was about $259,000,000, had fallen in 1893–94 to $200,000,000, a decrease of $59,000,000.

In Scotland during the same period the decrease in gross annual value exceeded $7,500,000. The reduction in the number of male wage-earners in agriculture in Great Britain between 1871 and 1891 was 187,356, the decrease in the first ten years of the period having been 105,414. In the number of female wage-earners the reduction between 1871 and 1881 was 16,385, and between 1881 and 1891 it was 38,312. In other words, while the total population of Great Britain rose in twenty years from 26,072,284 to 33,028,172, the number of the agricultural laborers fell from 1,161,738 to 919,685.

"As to the cause of the depression there is no disagreement on the part of the Commissioners. All ascribe it to the serious decline in the prices of farm produce, which in turn is imputed *directly to the pressure of foreign competition.* The Commissioners are unable to agree upon any remedy, but, on the contrary, look forward to a further reduction of the area of British land susceptible of profitable arable cultivation, together with a corresponding contraction of production and a diminution of the rural population."

In following the teachings of the Manchester school—in unduly developing her manufacturing interests at the expense of her agriculture—in studiously neglecting the best interests of her poor people—Great Britain has set a bad example to the rest of the world. No other country is now copying that example.

That England, Scotland, and Wales have made great progress during the Victorian era in many of the arts of an exalted civilization, and that many of their people are now better paid than when that era had its beginning, we are glad to record; but much of this progress has been gained despite the opposition of Britain's ruling classes; much of it is due to the general betterment of social conditions in all progressive countries resulting from the discovery of gold in California and Australia; much of it has resulted from the high standard of wages that has been established in our own country; much of it is the result of the scientific inventions of a wonderfully scientific age; and much of it is traceable to the influence of the freedom-loving spirit of the new era which was ushered in by the American and the French Revolutions. The fact remains, however, that the condition of the agricultural laborer, the coal miner, the factory hand, the iron worker, the man without a trade, and the great army of the unemployed is still hard and hopeless, while that of the London poor is pitiable and deplorable. All this has been true during the whole of Queen Victoria's long reign; it is true to-day. Mr. Gladstone and other Englishmen who believe in free trade should in all fairness tell the whole truth and not a part of it.

That Mr. Gladstone is not a correct reporter of current events and that it is possible for his prejudices to blind his judgment is illustrated by the great mistake he once made in forecasting the future of the Southern Confederacy. In a speech at Newcastle in October, 1862, Mr. Gladstone said: "We may have our own opinions about slavery; we may be for or against the South. But there is no doubt about this: Jefferson Davis and the other leaders of the South have made an army; they are making a navy; and they have made what is more than these—they have made a nation. *We may anticipate with certainty the success of the Southern States so far as regards their entire separation from the North.* I, for my own part, can not but believe that that event is as certain as any event yet future and contingent can be."

## CHAPTER VI.

### THE DESTRUCTION OF IRISH MANUFACTURES.

The hard treatment which Ireland has always received from England is a subject with which every student of history is more or less familiar; but every reader of history does not realize that the present impoverished condition of that unhappy country is mainly the result of a policy of repression and stamping out which England pursued toward the manufactures of Ireland in the sixteenth, seventeenth, and eighteenth centuries. The Right Hon. Sir John Barnard Byles, himself an Englishman, says that "for a long course of years Ireland's manufactures were systematically discouraged and stifled, while England's were, at the same time, protected and cherished."

There is a pitiful story told by Mr. Commissioner Mac Carthy, of Dublin, in *Harper's Monthly* for January, 1889, of the persistent and relentless efforts of the English Government to stamp out the woolen industry of Ireland. In the thirty-third year of the reign of Henry VIII. the importation of Irish woolen goods into England was prohibited. This legislation was re-enacted in the thirteenth year of the reign of Elizabeth, and afterwards, when Charles I. was on the throne, the exportation of Irish woolens to all countries was prohibited. In the closing years of the seventeenth century William III., in reply to addresses from both houses of the English Parliament, pledged himself "to do all that in him lay to discourage the woolen manufactures of Ireland," and true to this promise the exportation of woolen goods from Ireland was again prohibited by the English statute known as 10 and 11 William III., chapter 10. Mac Carthy says that "armed cruisers were stationed in Irish ports and seas to enforce this enactment." Edmund Burke says that "the whole woolen trade of Ireland, the natural staple of that kingdom, was deliberately destroyed." Mac Carthy adds that "other Irish industries followed the fate of the Irish woolen trade, the only notable exceptions being the linen trade of Ulster and the butter trade of the south." Dean Swift wrote in 1727: "Ireland is the only kingdom I ever heard or read of, either in ancient or modern story, which was denied the liberty of exporting their native commodities and manufactures wherever they pleased, except to countries at war with their own prince or State."

In the latter part of the eighteenth century, in 1779 and 1780, influenced probably by the successful revolt of the thirteen English colonies in America, these unjust restrictions were removed, and for a few years the manufacturing industries of Ireland prospered, but only for a few years. At the beginning of the present century, January 1, 1801, when the political union of Ireland with England was formally completed, provision was made in the Act of Union for gradually abrogating such measures of protection as had yet retained upon Irish soil a few of its important manufacturing industries. These measures of protection were the acts of the Irish Parliament, which the Act of Union provided should be gradually rendered null and void.

In 1822, protection having then been withdrawn from all Irish manufactures but not from *any* English manufactures, there was a famine in Ireland and great suffering resulted.

William Cobbett says that "there was food enough but no money to purchase it." Large numbers of the Irish people were without employment, through no fault of their own. Judge Byles, writing in 1849, states the effect of the abolition of Irish protective duties as follows: "Before the Union there were under protection Irish woolen manufactures, Irish carpet manufactures, Irish blanket manufactures, Irish silk manufactures, Irish calico manufactures, Irish flannel manufactures, and Irish stocking manufactures. *These manufactures are now smothered and extinct.*" English protected manufactures first crushed these Irish manufactures, and English free trade, permeating every Irish town and hamlet, next destroyed all hope of their recovery.

There is no sadder chapter in the industrial history of any nation than that which records the destruction of the manufactures of Ireland by the Act of Union of 1801, which united Ireland to Great Britain in a tighter bond than had previously existed, abolishing the Irish Parliament and obliterating the last vestige of Irish independence. The consummation of this measure of English greed and oppression was vigorously resisted by Irish statesmen, upon the ground, among other reasons, that it would destroy the manufactures of Ireland, which were then in a flourishing condition. The protest of the Irish House of Commons against the proposed Act of Union is one of the most eloquent and pitiful protests against the perpetration of a political crime that is to be found in the annals of any oppressed people. In literary merit it is not surpassed by our own Declaration of Independence. Its reference to the destruction of Irish manufactures which would be certain to follow the adoption of the Act of Union is in the following words:

"In manufactures any attempt it makes to offer any benefit which we do not now enjoy is vain and delusive, and wherever it is to have effect that effect will be to our injury; most of the duties on imports which operate as protections to our manufactures are under its provisions either to be removed or reduced immediately, and those which will be reduced are to cease entirely at a limited time, though many of our manufactures owe their existence to the protection of those duties, and though it is not in the power of human wisdom to foresee any precise time when they may be able to thrive without them. Your Majesty's faithful Commons feel more than an ordinary interest in laying this fact before you, because they have under your Majesty's approbation raised up and nursed many of those manufactures, and by so doing have encouraged much capital to be vested in them, the proprietors of which are now to be left unprotected and to be deprived of the Parliament on whose faith they embarked themselves, their families, and properties in the undertaking."

The conclusion of the protest of the House of Commons is in the following eloquent words: "We feel it our bounden duty to ourselves, our country, and our posterity to lay this our most solemn protest and prayer before your Majesty, that you will be graciously pleased to extend your paternal protection to your faithful and loyal subjects, and to save them from the danger threatened by your Majesty's ministers in this their ruinous and destructive project, humbly declaring, with the most cordial and warm sincerity, that we are actuated therein by an irresistible sense of duty, by an unshaken loyalty to your Majesty, by a veneration for the British name, by an ardent attachment to the British nation with whom we have so often declared we will stand or fall, and by a determination to preserve forever the connection between the two kingdoms on which the happiness, the power, and the strength of each irrevocably and unalterably depend."

The protest of the Irish Peers, after reciting the evils which the proposed measure would entail upon Ireland and the dishonorable means resorted to by the British Government to secure its adoption, concludes as follows: "Against all these, and the fatal consequences they may produce, we have endeavored to interpose our votes, and failing we transmit to after times our names in solemn protest on behalf of the parliamentary constitution of this realm, the liberty which it secured, the trade which it protected, the connection which it preserved, and the constitution which it supplied and fortified: this we feel ourselves called upon to do in support of our characters, our honor, and whatever is left to us [that is] worthy to be transmitted to our posterity."

The results to Irish manufactures of the free trade between the two countries which the Act of Union established have justified all the fears of Irish statesmen. With the sole exception of the linen manufacture, for which the Irish climate is especially adapted, these manufactures have virtually perished. The Irish people, denied by free trade the privilege of engaging in manufacturing enterprises, have for nearly a century been almost entirely restricted to small farming as a means of maintaining an existence, and the lands they have tilled they have been compelled to rent from exacting landlords, without hope of ever being able to own them. In a speech at Portland, Maine, in 1886, Mr. Blaine said that 729 Englishmen own one-half the land in Ireland and that 3,000 other men own most of the other half. Exclusive devotion to agriculture under unfavorable conditions has wrought the inevitable results of poverty and decadence. The population of Ireland has declined; famine has followed famine; unable to live at home the Irish people have been forced to emigrate to more hospitable lands, and particularly to our own land, although there is not a people on earth who are more attached to the land of their birth. In 1841 the population of Ireland was 8,199,853; in 1871, through famine and emigration, it had fallen to 5,412,377; in 1891 it was only 4,704,750. Famine and emigration in a land capable of supporting twenty millions of people might have been prevented in large part if not wholly if Irish manufactures had been preserved and fostered. But England decreed their destruction and this it has accomplished, as the following circumstantial statements will abundantly testify.

In a speech delivered in Ireland in 1848 that patriotic Irishman, Thomas Francis Meagher, said: "The cotton manufactures of Dublin, which employed 14,000 operatives, have been destroyed; the stuff and serge manufactures, which employed 1,491 operatives, have been destroyed; the calico looms of Balbriggan have been destroyed; the flannel manufacture of Rathdrum has been destroyed; the blanket manufacture of Kilkenny has been destroyed; the camlet trade of Bandon, which produced £100,000 a year, has been destroyed; the worsted and stuff manufactures of Waterford have been destroyed; the ratteen and frieze manufactures of Carrick-on-Suir have been destroyed."

In an article in *The American*, of Philadelphia, in 1886, its editor, Robert Ellis Thompson, said: "In ten years [following the Act of Union] the exports of woolen drapery fell from 360,000 yards to 20,000 yards, while the imports rose from 600,000 yards to 2,400,000 yards. By 1823 the export was at an end, but the import stood at 2,500,000 yards. But as late as 1822 two-thirds in value or one-half in amount of the woolen cloth used in Ireland was still made at home, while a population of 35,000 derived support from the industry. By 1850 the number employed was only 625, and the increase of recent years has brought this up only to 2,022 in 1879. The first mill for cotton was built in 1784, and by the date of the Union this industry gave employment to 13,500 persons. By 1817 the number thus employed was but 12,091, although the 68 per cent. duties were not taken off till 1816. By 1850 it had declined to 2,937 persons, and by 1861 to 2,734 persons. In 1879 the number was 1,620."

For many years Mr. Gladstone and other English statesmen have advocated the restoration of home rule to Ireland. But home rule would avail but little to Ireland unless it were accompanied by a restoration of protective duties for the benefit of Irish industries, and this boon Mr. Gladstone, who is a free trader, has never offered.

# CHAPTER VII.

## AN IMPERIAL BRITISH ZOLLVEREIN.

FREE TRADE is not accepted by all the British people as a wise economic policy for their country. There is to-day an aggressive party in Great Britain which believes in "fair trade," which is only another name for old-time protection, and there is a larger party which advocates the creation of a British zollverein, with the object of reviving protective duties against all countries except Great Britain and her colonies. But the attempt to establish a customs-union, or zollverein, discriminating in tariff rates against other countries but maintaining absolute free trade between the members of the union, will fail for many reasons if it is earnestly pressed. The policy indicated is urged partly to appease British agricultural interests, which are clamoring loudly for protection against foreign competition. It will fail for the following reasons:

It would be resisted by many of the colonies because it would prevent them from developing their own industries by protective duties, and because it would prevent them from raising at the custom-house the revenue that they would need. In Canada, for instance, the Protectionists, or Nationalists, have been strong enough for many years to control the government. They are at present out of power, but their successors have not proposed free trade or any policy approaching it. One of the Australian colonies, Victoria, is also strongly wedded to the protective policy.

Discriminating against other countries would cause some of the colonies, if not all of them, to lose valuable trade with those countries, which might be expected to buy sparingly of British colonial products if their own products were not taken in at least partial exchange. The ships of foreign countries would have less occasion to visit colonial ports than they now have. The foreign commerce of the colonies with countries other than the mother country would certainly decline.

Countries discriminated against would retaliate by adopting discriminating duties of their own. If Canada, as an illustration, were to discriminate through the proposed zollverein against the United States and in favor of Great Britain the United States would certainly find a way to check the imports of Canadian products into United States markets. Canada would be a heavy loser by the zollverein. She would not increase greatly, if at all, her exports to the other members of the zollverein, while she would certainly export less of her products to the United States, which now takes annually about thirty per cent. of her total exports. Her present discriminating tariff bodes her no good.

If the colonies were compelled by discriminating duties to trade more and more with Great Britain and less and less with other countries they would soon find themselves at the mercy of British manufacturers, who would have a virtual monopoly of their markets and would regulate their prices accordingly. The colonies would not welcome this monopoly, especially as it would be accompanied by a blow at their own manufacturing industries.

Great Britain herself, by discriminating in favor of her colonies and against foreign countries, would not then any more than now come anywhere near supplying her own wants for agricultural and other products. She would still be largely dependent on other countries for wheat, flour, beef, pork, petroleum, cotton, sugar, and many other articles which are consumed in the daily life of her people or are essential to the prosperity of her manufacturing industries. Would her people be willing to pay duties on these products which are now free and which her colonies could not furnish in sufficient quantities to meet her wants, even if other countries would not increase their duties on British products entering their markets? Would the workingmen of England, Scotland, Wales, and Ireland be willing, for instance, to have the cost of their loaf of bread coming from the United States increased for the benefit of the wheat growers of India or the wheat growers at home? Or would the cotton manufacturers of Manchester be willing to pay a duty on cotton coming from the United States that the growing of cotton in India might be stimulated? There would be both bread and cotton riots if these innovations were attempted.

But, supposing that the British people were willing to try the experiment of imposing duties on the products of other countries which come in competition with the products of British colonies, the increased cost of food and of the raw materials of British manufacturing industries would enhance the cost of British manufactured products. The increased cost of food would compel the payment of higher wages. With a higher labor cost and a higher cost of raw materials than now prevail, and the consequent higher cost of manufactured products, the markets for these products would everywhere be narrowed, even in the colonies. British manufacturers would surely be losers by a discriminating policy.

The fact that land in the British Islands is owned by the aristocratic class and can not to any considerable extent be purchased by any other class will of itself prevent the adoption of a discriminating policy for the benefit of British agricultural interests, notwithstanding the undoubted fact that the tenant farmers and the farm laborers of Great Britain are richly deserving of sympathy and of protection against foreign competition. Why should the poor men of England, Scotland, Ireland, and Wales distress themselves for the benefit of the landed aristocracy? The aristocratic ownership of land in Great Britain constitutes, indeed, the weakest feature of the whole scheme to revive the protective policy in that country, either through a zollverein or otherwise.

Lastly, the zollverein project proposes in effect the abandonment of British free trade for the benefit primarily of British agriculture but also in the hope that other British industries would be benefited. But even if Great Britain should now abandon her free trade policy she would gain nothing. It is too late for her to retrace the steps by which fifty years ago she abandoned her agriculture to its fate that she might manufacture for all the world cotton and woolen goods, iron and steel, and other products of her factories and workshops. She should have adhered to a policy of moderate protection for both her agriculture and her manufactures, developing both side by side and neither at the expense of the other. She chose the unwise part. Her agriculture is now and long has been greatly depressed, and at last her manufacturing supremacy is successfully assailed in every branch by countries which, in self-defense against her aggressive policy, were compelled to develop their own industrial resources by protective tariffs.

## CHAPTER VIII.

#### BRITISH STEAMSHIP SUBSIDIES.

The protective policy is still retained in those acts of the British Parliament which every year grant large subsidies to British steamship companies, enabling them to carry the manufactures of Great Britain to every port in the world in competition with other nations. These subsidies are attended with many important benefits to British trade.

In 1871 Judge Kelley said: "England's enormous annual subsidies to steamship companies are part of an ingenious system of protection by which she hopes to maintain a monopoly of shipbuilding and the carrying trade. She thus pays part of the freight on foreign raw materials used by her manufacturers and the fabrics and wares they export. These subsidies amounted last year, as was stated by the Chancellor of the Exchequer in his speech of April 20, 1871, when presenting to Parliament his budget for this year, to £1,225,000, or over $6,000,000."

In 1885 John Roach said that from 1827 to 1840 England's carrying trade went from bad to worse, and that in 1837 "she began the policy of subsidy, straight-out subsidy. Samuel Cunard offered in 1840 to build a line of mail steamships for the North Atlantic, and his offer was at once accepted." Mr. Roach then states that Mr. Cunard built four side-wheel ocean steamers, and that he "got his contract of $413,000 the first year, and this was increased to $550,000 the next year, or 70 per cent. per annum on the whole cost of the ships. This was a subsidy, pure and simple, given to Mr. Cunard to enable him to establish and maintain his line, and increased that he might run his line not only without loss but at a profit."

Mr. Roach further said in 1885: "In a report of the Postmaster General, dated July 20, 1870, I find this significant passage: 'By the terms of the contract concluded with the Peninsular and Oriental Steam Navigation Company on the 19th of November, 1867, the *subsidy* to be paid the company is set down at £400,000 ($2,000,000) a year, with a stipulation, on the one hand, that whenever the annual income of the company from all sources does not admit of the payment of a dividend of 8 per cent. on the capital employed the *subsidy* shall be increased by so much—subject to a limit of £100,000 ($500,000)—as is required to make up such a dividend.' Here is not only a subsidy but a government guarantee of an 8 per cent. dividend to the company's stockholders."

The Glasgow *Herald* for September 24, 1892, contains an elaborate article on "the balance-sheet of an Atlantic liner," in which, after summing up the cost of running these large vessels and the income from freight and passengers, the writer admits in the following words the direct payment of subsidies: "Another source of income in these large steamers is the cruiser subvention from the Admiralty. This equals from £17,000 to £18,000 per annum. For this sum the companies are prepared on an outbreak of war to hand over their ships to act as armed cruisers, for which of course they would then be handsomely paid. The *Teutonic* and *Majestic* have guns to be in readiness, and on high occasions these have been mounted. *Then, again, there is the income from the mails.*"

The same paper for December 17, 1894, said: "In 1840 the Cunard Line, or, as it was then styled, the British and North American Royal Mail Steam Packet Company, was formed. It was to conduct a fortnightly steam mail service between Liverpool, Halifax, and Boston, and the contract under which it served was for seven years. Seven years later the expansion of the trade with the States forced the British Government to double the mail service, and with its *subsidy* increased from £81,000 to £173,340 per annum the Cunard Company undertook the work. Since then the service has, with the exception of a momentary break in 1889, been continuous."

In commenting on the passage by Congress in 1891 of the Postal Subsidy bill the London *Engineering* for March 13, 1891, says: "The Senate and the House of Representatives, which constitute the legislative houses of America, have passed what is called the Postal Subsidy bill, which may be more accurately described as a bill to subsidize American-built steamers. Originally there were two bills before the Legislature, one of which gave bounties for shipbuilding and the other subsidies for the carrying of mails. The subsidy was based on the mile run of the steamers, *and it differs from that paid by this country* in respect that the vessel must be of American build."

We could cite other proofs of the practice of the British Government to subsidize its steamship lines. The subsidies above referred to were paid for mail service, these subsidies being largely repaid by the mail receipts on foreign and colonial postage. This superior mail service helps British trade in various ways, in addition to furnishing quick transportation for the products of British workshops.

Hon. William F. Prosser explains as follows in *The United Service Magazine* for April, 1896, the benefits which are thus reaped by British trade: "The policy of Great Britain has not only enabled her to increase her shipping industries and operations immensely, but, as she thus secures control of the mail service, she, at the same time, largely increases her mercantile and banking business, because merchants all over the world prefer to do their trading where the mail facilities are of the best character. Her steamers everywhere make it a point to accommodate their arrivals and departures to the convenience of the mail service. It is not unusual for English steamers to wait a day or two in foreign ports for the mails in order that British merchants may get the benefit of mercantile orders."

Germany, France, and Italy have copied Great Britain's example in subsidizing mail steamship companies, and our own country has recently timidly entered upon a similar policy. We commend most earnestly this British policy. This country needs subsidized steamship lines to increase its export trade a hundred times more than it needs reciprocity treaties. But this British policy is not a free trade policy, but a policy of protection. Great Britain can not with any show of consistency pretend that she has abandoned the protective policy so long as she pays large subsidies annually to her mail steamship companies for the extension, among other things, of British trade.

Colonel Prosser gives the following list of British and Continental steamship companies, with the number of their steamers, which are subsidized to a greater or less extent, the aggregate amounting to millions of dollars annually. The British India Company, 103 steamers; Peninsular and

Oriental, 36 steamers; Messageries Maritimes, 61 steamers; North German Lloyd's, 66 steamers; Navigationze Generale, 106 steamers; Compagnie Generale Transatlantique, 66 steamers; Hamburg-America, 86 steamers; Wilson Line, 86 steamers; Austrian Lloyd's, 73 steamers; White Star Line, 20 steamers; Cunard Line, 26 steamers. The United States pays in 1897 a mail subsidy to *four* Atlantic steamships, the *New York, Paris, St. Paul,* and *St. Louis,* of the American Line, this subsidy having been provided for in the Postal Subsidy bill already referred to.

There is a Bureau of American Republics at Washington, and much is said in its publications and elsewhere about the necessity of extending our trade with all Central and South American countries, but not one vessel has been subsidized by our Government to carry even the mails to these countries. If we had adopted the policy of subsidizing mail steamship lines between our principal ports and the principal ports of Central and South America our export trade to those countries would now rapidly increase. Trade would follow the flag. But to-day, when we sell a steel bridge to one of our South American neighbors, it must first be sent to Liverpool and thence to its destination. The missing link in our export trade of all kinds is direct steam communication with all parts of the world. With this link supplied there would be no temptation to compromise our protective tariff professions or to annoy friendly nations by injecting into our tariff legislation the thoroughly British policy of commercial treaties and so-called reciprocity. Our low prices and the excellent quality of our products would do the rest. They are accomplishing wonders as things are.

# CHAPTER IX.

### TARIFF LEGISLATION FROM WASHINGTON TO McKINLEY.

IN the early days of the great American Republic the principle of protection to home industry was fully recognized. Nearly all the great men who aided in securing our political independence were protectionists. Washington, Adams, Jefferson, Madison, Hamilton, Franklin, and others advocated the protective policy with more or less earnestness. The necessity of securing greatly needed protection for our manufacturing industries and thereby promoting "the general welfare" was one of the principal reasons for the adoption of the Constitution of 1787, which established "a more perfect Union" than had existed under the Articles of Confederation. In an address to the citizens of Buffalo, New York, in June, 1833, Daniel Webster said: "The protection of American labor against the injurious competition of foreign labor, so far at least as respects general handicraft productions, is known historically to have been one end designed to be obtained by establishing the Constitution."

The first petition that was presented to the First Congress, in March, 1789, before Washington's inauguration, emanated from over seven hundred mechanics and other citizens of "the town of Baltimore," who prayed that Congress would render the country "independent in fact as well as in name" by imposing protective duties on foreign manufactures. Other petitions of like character were presented from citizens of Boston, New York, Philadelphia, Charleston, and other places. Within two days after the Presidential vote was counted Mr. Madison introduced in the House of Representatives a bill embodying the views of the petitioners. That bill became a law; it was our first protective tariff; and it was the first act of general legislation passed under the new Constitution of the United States. As stated in its preamble it was enacted because it was "*necessary* for the support of the Government, for the discharge of the debts of the United States, *and the encouragement and protection of manufactures.*" It became a law by the signature of Washington on the 4th day of July, 1789.

The policy of protection which was embodied in the tariff act of 1789 was continued in subsequent tariff legislation. The fact is worthy of note that a clause in one of the earliest of our tariffs provided a duty of three cents a pound on raw cotton for the protection of our new cotton-growing industry. On December 5, 1791, Alexander Hamilton, the Secretary of the Treasury, presented a report to Congress which contained a plea for protection to American industry which is yet regarded as the most philosophical and statesmanlike argument in behalf of the protective policy that has ever emanated from the pen of an American writer. Senator John P. Jones, of Nevada, is entitled to the thanks of the present generation of American protectionists for presenting in the Senate of the United States on September 10, 1890, the most philosophical argument in behalf of the same policy that has appeared since Hamilton's report. Both arguments are masterpieces.

Mr. Blaine says that "important and radical additions to the revenue system promptly followed Mr. Hamilton's recommendations. From that time onward, for a period of more than twenty years, additional tariff laws were passed by each succeeding Congress, modifying and generally increasing the rate of duties first imposed and adding many new articles to the dutiable list."

Although intended to be fully protective of our infant manufactures the early tariff acts were in fact only slightly so. Duties generally did not range above 15 per cent. The disparity between our people and those of Europe in capital and skill and other resources was too great to be overcome by the low duties that were imposed. England supplied us with most of our manufactured goods, and to repress our rising industries she offered many of these goods at unremunerative prices. "An immense quantity of merchandise was introduced into the country. English goods were sold at lower rates in our maritime cities than at Liverpool or London." We were still the commercial colony of Great Britain.

In addition to throwing her cheap goods upon our markets Great Britain continued the policy she had adopted before the Revolution of imposing severe restrictions upon the exportation of machines and tools used in manufactures and upon the emigration of her skilled workmen. Heavy penalties were enforced for "the enticing of artificers or workmen in the iron and steel manufactures out of the kingdom and the exportation of any tools used in these branches to any place beyond the seas." Other industries were dealt with in like manner.

At the beginning of our last war with Great Britain, in 1812, all duties were doubled, with the twofold purpose of increasing the revenues and stimulating manufactures. This legislation remained unaltered until 1816, and while it was in force every existing industry in the country was quickened into new life and many new industries were created. There was indeed great need of an industrial awakening. "The war of 1812 found us without manufactures and without machinery. Our people were without the means of producing clothing for their armies or the material of war." But in 1816 duties were generally reduced, although the tariff of that year was intended to afford ample protection. It is a strange coincidence that it was in this very year that Lord Brougham declared that "it was well worth while to incur a loss upon the first exportation, in order by the glut to *stifle in the cradle* those rising manufactures in the United States which the war has forced into existence contrary to the natural course of things."

From 1816 to 1824 none of our manufacturing industries were sufficiently protected, and British manufacturers held almost complete possession of our markets. Again we were the commercial colony of Great Britain. Inadequate duties favored her ambition, but she had other advantages in competing with our infant manufactures besides the encouragement extended to her by our timid tariff legislation. In May, 1868, *The League*, a newspaper published in New York, and the organ at that time of American free traders, referring to British manufactures from 1816 to 1824, said that among their advantages was "the great advantage of being already established, with machinery all built, trade all regulated, and in the midst of a superabundant supply of labor, which had no competing opening, and which could therefore be had for the asking, *at the lowest wages on which people could live.*"

The period intervening between the close of the last war with Great Britain and the year 1824 is frequently referred to as "the era of good feeling" in our political history, but it was an era of discouragement and disaster in our industrial history. The unchecked importation of foreign goods was the main cause of the industrial depression and financial ruin which marked that gloomy period. In Bishop's *History of American Manufactures* we find a melancholy picture of the condition of the country in 1819. This excellent authority says: "A general paralysis now fell upon all branches of industry. The distress became more general and severe than had ever been known, and but little alleviation was experienced for several years to come. The banks suffered from lack of specie. Bankruptcies overtook the mercantile and shipping interests, whose merchandise lay on their hands, and whose ships could neither be employed nor sold save at ruinous losses. Rents and the value of all real estate were enormously depreciated. Farms were mortgaged or sold at one-half and one-third their value. Factories and workshops were everywhere closed. Manufacturers were forced to abandon extensive and flourishing establishments, reared as if by magic in the last few years, and with their operatives and multitudes of handicraft workmen entered into competition with the cultivators of the soil and swelled the products of agricultural labor, for which there was no longer a market."

On the 11th of February, 1824, in the House of Representatives, the effect of the tariff of 1816 upon the manufactures of the country was stated as follows by Mr. Tod, of Pennsylvania: "The tariff of 1816 had been inadequate. Under it the newly-erected manufactures of earthenware had been the first to disappear. They and their workmen were no more talked of than if they had never existed. In the same way went the most of our glass factories, our manufactures of white and black lead, our woolens, our hemp. Domestic iron had lingered awhile longer, and still held a feeble existence, dwindling every year, and gradually sinking under foreign importations. All the devastations and losses of the war had been nothing compared with the devastations and losses of manufacturing capital under the tariff of 1816."

On the 28th of February, 1824, James Buchanan, who was then a Representative in Congress from Pennsylvania, thus alluded to the prostrated condition of the iron industry in those eastern districts of his State which were open to foreign competition: "Although that portion of Pennsylvania abounds with ore, with wood, and with water power, yet its manufactories generally have sunk into ruin and exist only as standing monuments of the false policy of the Government. The manufacturers and their laborers have both been thrown out of employment and the neighboring farmer is without a market." It was in this year that General Jackson wrote his celebrated letter to Dr. Coleman advocating the continuance and enlargement of the protective policy. General Jackson had previously written to General Robert Patterson, of Philadelphia, on May 17, 1823, as follows: "Upon the success of our manufactures, as the handmaid of agriculture and commerce, depends in a great measure the independence of our country."

In a memorable speech in the Senate in 1832 Henry Clay thus characterized the period between 1816 and 1824: "If I were to select any term of seven years since the adoption of the present Constitution which exhibited a scene of the most widespread dismay and desolation it would be exactly that term of seven years which immediately preceded the establishment of the tariff of 1824."

The tariff of 1824 gave a new impetus to enterprise and greatly promoted the general prosperity. It was the first thoroughly protective tariff enacted by Congress in a time of peace. In 1828 the duties on iron and steel, carpets, blankets, other woolen goods, edged tools, hemp, flax, and many other articles were still further increased. The Legislature of New York this year, by an almost unanimous vote, passed resolutions recommending iron to the protection of Congress.

The beneficial effects of the protective tariffs of 1824 and 1828 are stated in the following extract from the speech of Mr. Clay, already quoted: "If the term of seven years were to be selected of the greatest prosperity which this people have enjoyed since the establishment of their present Constitution it would be exactly that period of seven years which immediately followed the passage of the tariff of 1824. This transformation of the condition of the country from gloom and distress to brightness and prosperity has been mainly the work of American legislation fostering American industry, instead of allowing it to be controlled by foreign legislation cherishing foreign industry."

The general tariff act of 1832 made some changes in duties, but its principal purpose was to reaffirm the policy of protection in the most positive terms. In discussing the bill in the House of Representatives Mr. Crawford and Mr. Stewart, of Pennsylvania, bore additional testimony to the good results which had followed the passage of the acts of 1824 and 1828. Mr. Crawford said: "Manufactories have sprung up throughout the country, not in one town, not in one district, but everywhere, and, like the dews and rains and sunshine from heaven, stimulating everything and furnishing food for everybody." Mr. Stewart said that the country "had risen to its present high and palmy state of public prosperity" under the protective system—"a system which has vindicated its adoption by all its fruits." Mr. Davis, of Massachusetts, referring to the tariff legislation of the First Congress, also said : "The act which laid the foundation of the Great American policy infused the vital principle into the drooping, disheartened spirits of all laborers. It restored a discontented community to tranquillity, and caused peace and happiness to pervade this widespread country."

But, in 1833, influenced purely by political considerations growing out of Southern hostility to the protective policy, Congress exchanged this policy for one which provided for a gradual reduction of duties on foreign imports from and after December 31, 1833, to continue until December 31, 1842, after which date they should be succeeded by a uniform duty of twenty per cent. The tariff of 1833 is known as the Henry Clay compromise tariff. Henry Clay once told a Pennsylvania iron manufacturer who is still living that the tariff of 1833 was "a mistake." It is a singular fact that the gradual abandonment of protective duties which was provided for in the tariff of 1833 did not very greatly differ in one particular from the provision in the Act of Union of 1801 abolishing Irish independence, which decreed that all protective duties on Irish manufactures should be gradually reduced and finally cease at the end of certain specified years in the near future. Under the operation of the compromise tariff of 1833 imports steadily increased and all our industries were greatly prostrated.

The disastrous consequences of the tariff of 1833 culminated in 1837 in one of the severest financial panics in our history, and the five years immediately following that event were indeed hard times for the American farmer and workingman. The reader of advanced years will remember that in those years the farmer sold his corn and apples and potatoes for twelve and a half cents a bushel, and that a cow and calf in the spring of the year would bring only seven or eight dollars. Agricultural products were rarely sold for cash, but were taken to the country stores and exchanged for English axes, hatchets, saws, calicoes, and other articles of foreign manufacture, for which exorbitant prices were charged. Turnpike companies, small municipalities, and other employers of labor met their obligations with printed due-bills, or "scrip," which passed into general circulation. Domestic manufacturers very generally put out their fires, and their foreign competitors again possessed the American market. Labor was nowhere in demand. It was a period of complete prostration and widespread disaster. The Treasury of the United States was almost bankrupted.

The tariff of 1842 again placed the policy of protection in the ascendant, and while it lasted business revived and the country prospered. The Treasury was replenished. In 1846 duties were again reduced by a tariff act framed by Robert J. Walker, President Polk's Secretary of the Treasury. Mr. Polk had been elected to the Presidency in 1844 upon the deceptive plea that he " was as good a tariff man as Henry Clay." Pennsylvania was carried for him with the shibboleth, " Polk, Dallas, and Shunk, and the tariff of 1842." Notwithstanding the stimulating effects produced by the Irish famine, the discovery of gold in California, and the Crimean war the country did not prosper under the tariff of 1846. Agriculture flourished only while the Irish famine and the Crimean war lasted, and the gold of California was exported to pay for the products of European workshops. Our iron industry, which had been greatly stimulated under the tariff of 1842, met with disastrous reverses. The tariff of 1846 was a tariff for revenue only. The prevailing rate was 30 per cent. ad valorem.

With a strange fatuity Congress adopted in 1857 still further modifications of the tariff in the interest of foreign manufacturers and the panic of that year was one of the consequences. The legislation of 1857 is known as the James Guthrie tariff. The prevailing rate was 24 per cent. ad valorem. The years 1857, 1858, 1859, and 1860 were four of the most discouraging years in our industrial history. Many banks and manufacturing companies failed. A leading iron manufacturing firm in Pennsylvania paid its workmen in "scrip," or store orders, during the whole four years. The Treasury of the United States also suffered from insufficient revenue, and the Government was compelled in a time of peace to borrow money to meet its ordinary expenses.

So prostrated had the country become in consequence of the legislation of 1846 and 1857 that a return to the policy of generous protection was rendered absolutely necessary, and this was accomplished by the passage in 1861 of the Morrill tariff bill. This bill was not a war measure, as has been erroneously inferred from its date. It was reported to the House of Representatives on March 12, 1860, and it passed that body on May 10. It passed the Senate on February 27, 1861, and it was approved by President Buchanan on March 2. It took effect on April 1. The new tariff formed the first in an unbroken series of protective tariff acts extending over a long period and ending with the Mc-

Kinley tariff of 1890. To the wisdom which inspired and maintained these enactments do we owe the wonderful prosperity of the country from 1861 to 1893—prosperity achieved despite the destruction occasioned by a great civil war and despite the hardships attending the shrinkage of values and the checking of all enterprise which followed the Jay Cooke panic of September 18, 1873.

For the first time in its history there was inserted in the platform of the Republican party in 1860 a resolution approving the protective policy, and this indorsement of that policy aided greatly in securing Abraham Lincoln's election to the Presidency in that year. It secured to him the electoral vote of Pennsylvania. The resolution was as follows: "That, while providing revenue for the support of the General Government by duties upon imports, sound policy requires such an adjustment of these imposts as to encourage the development of the industrial interests of the whole country; and we commend that policy of national exchanges which secures to the workingmen liberal wages, to agriculture remunerative prices, to mechanics and manufacturers an adequate reward for their skill, labor, and enterprise, and to the nation commercial prosperity and independence." Mr. Lincoln was himself a firm believer in the protective policy. On October 11, 1859, he wrote to Edward Wallace: "I was an old Henry Clay Tariff Whig. In old times I made more speeches on that subject than any other. I have not since changed my views."

Soon after the second elevation of Mr. Cleveland to the Presidency, in 1893, there ensued a great panic, followed by a great depression in all industrial enterprises, caused by a lack of confidence by business men in the financial situation and by the general expectation that the tariff would again be revised in the interest of foreign manufacturers, both the legislative and executive branches of the Government having again passed into the hands of the advocates of a tariff for revenue only. The financial and industrial depression of 1893 and 1894 was very great. Many banks and manufacturing companies failed. Wages were reduced and many workingmen were thrown out of employment. There was never in this country such a summer of depression and prostration as that of 1893. On November 1, 1893, the silver-purchase provision of the Sherman act of 1890 was repealed, but an improvement in business did not follow this legislation. Many persons had predicted a different result.

The expected revision of the tariff happened in 1894, when the Wilson tariff bill, the original of which was modeled after the Walker tariff of 1846, became a law on August 28th. The enactment of the Wilson tariff in 1894 was followed by a partial return of business confidence and by a revival in 1895 of activity in the iron trade and in some other industries, due partly to the fact that the question of tariff revision had been settled, even if wrongly settled, and partly to the fact that the financial tension caused by the panic had been largely relieved. But there was no general revival of prosperity, and in a few months, beginning with the early part of 1896, all business was as bad as it had been in 1893 and 1894. Wages were further reduced. Duties in the Wilson tariff were, as a rule, too low to give needed encouragement and protection to domestic industries. This depressing and discouraging condition of affairs continued throughout all of 1896 and in 1897 down to the enactment of an entirely new tariff, known as the Dingley tariff, which was framed wholly on protectionist lines, and which became a law on July 24th of the last named year. The depression was intensified in 1896 by the Democratic and Populistic uprising of that year in favor of the free coinage of silver and by the widespread manifestations of discontent with the low prices of agricultural products and with other undesirable conditions, for which it was declared the free coinage of silver would be a sure remedy. Fortunately this view did not prevail at the Presidential and Congressional elections of that year, William McKinley being elected to the Presidency on a platform committed to the gold standard and the restoration of the protective policy. The political complexion of the new Congress was also in harmony with this platform.

With the enactment of the Dingley tariff, which was passed at a special session of the new Congress, all our industries at once revived. Confidence was completely restored, and on every hand the fact was recognized that during the remainder of President McKinley's term, if not longer, the country's markets would be secured to our own people and its finances would rest on a secure foundation. But it must be frankly added that the revival of prosperity following the enactment of the new tariff was greatly promoted by the fortuitous circumstance that there was an extraordinary foreign demand in 1897 for our agricultural products, of which, happily, the year's harvests gave us a large surplus. Wheat rose to over a dollar a bushel. Railroad securities advanced in price, employment for labor was more general, the demand for manufactured products increased, and there was a slight improvement in the prices obtained for them. The year 1897 closed with the country again prosperous in every channel.

## CHAPTER X.

### THE TARIFFS OF 1842, 1846, AND 1857.

THE protective tariff of 1842 became a law by the signature of President Tyler on August 30 of that year. Its influence upon the prosperity of the country is explained in the following extract from the annual message of President Tyler in December, 1844: "The credit of the Government, which had experienced a temporary embarrassment, has been thoroughly restored. Its coffers, which for a season were empty, have been replenished. A currency, nearly uniform in its value, has taken the place of one depreciated and almost worthless. Commerce and manufactures, which had suffered in common with every other interest, have once more revived, and the whole country exhibits an aspect of prosperity and happiness." This beneficent measure was succeeded by the revenue tariff of 1846, which received the signature of President Polk on July 30 of that year.

The widely different effects upon all the industries of the country of the tariffs of 1842 and 1846 may be inferred from their influence upon the prosperity of the iron trade. The former, as has been stated, was a protective tariff and the latter a tariff for revenue only. Under the operation of the compromise tariff of 1833 the production of pig iron in this country had fallen in 1842 to less than 230,000 tons. The tariff of 1842 so stimulated the iron industry that the production in 1846 was estimated by Robert J. Walker to amount to 765,000 tons; in 1847 and 1848, the impetus given to the iron industry by the tariff of 1842 having been checked by the tariff of 1846, the production of pig iron increased but slightly, reaching about 800,000 tons annually; in 1849 it fell to about 650,000 tons; in 1850 the census showed a still further reduction to 563,755 tons. The production continued to decline until 1853, the production in 1852 not exceeding 500,000 tons. In 1853 it began to increase, in consequence chiefly of the increased demand for iron for railway construction, but the increase was slow, and in 1857 and 1858 production again declined. The direct effect of the tariff of 1846 was to seriously check the production of domestic pig iron and to close many furnaces. Robert J. Walker's estimate of 765,000 tons in 1846 corresponds almost exactly with the actual production of 788,515 tons in 1856—ten years later. In 1860, the last year of a tariff for revenue only, we made only 821,223 tons.

In 1842 our total imports of pig iron from all countries amounted to 18,694 tons; in 1846 they increased to only 24,187 tons; in 1848 they rose to 51,632 tons; in 1849 to 105,632 tons; in 1850, 1851, and 1852 they averaged 77,000 tons; in 1853 they rose to 114,227 tons; and in 1854 to 160,484 tons. Secretary Walker's policy worked well, therefore, in increasing enormously our imports of pig iron.

In a communication to the New York *Journal of Commerce*, written on December 26, 1849, Cooper & Hewitt, of New York, showed the paralyzing effects of the tariff of 1846 upon the whole American iron trade. We quote from this letter the following specific statements.

"What is the real condition of the domestic iron trade? There are one or two positions in the country which combine such extraordinary natural advantages with every superior quality as to make them almost independent of legislation; but as to the *great fact* that the great majority of establishments, judiciously located and managed with proper skill and economy, have been compelled to suspend work, throughout the land, for want of remunerating work there can not be a shadow of doubt. . . . A few merchant mills are also kept in motion from the absolute necessity of having a certain amount of iron of superior quality for fine work; *but of fifteen rail mills only two are in operation, doing partial work*, and that only because their inland position secured them against foreign competition for the limited orders of neighboring railroads, *and when these are executed not a single rail mill will be at work in the land.*"

The following letter, written from Brooklyn, New York, by W. J. Parsons, on February 15, 1882, and addressed to the Secretary of the American Iron and Steel Association, shows how the consumers of iron rails in our country were injured after 1849 by the interrupted development of the domestic rail industry, and it shows, too, who were benefited. This letter confirms with curious and pathetic exactness the correctness of Cooper & Hewitt's prediction in that year that every rail mill in the country would soon be closed.

"About the year 1850 the writer was a clerk in a house in Boston which represented one of the largest of the English iron rolling mills. It was a period of low duties on railroad iron; I think 30 per cent. ad valorem was the rate, under the act of 1846. The United States rail market was supplied partly from England and partly from American mills. The prices of rails were very low, and the English houses persisted in constantly depressing them, until, as this squeezing process went on, the American mills gradually shut down, and finally the last American mill was closed. When the news from our house went across to England that there was no longer any danger from American competition the reply immediately came back, '*Advance prices.*' This process of advancing prices then went on, until within less than a year prices to the American consumers had gone up nearly or quite 100 per cent.—far beyond the price at which the home industries would gladly have supplied the demand had they been at work."

Our iron rail industry made a brave effort, however, to recover from the paralyzing effects of the tariff of 1846, but how seriously it was handicapped by foreign competition will be seen by a study of the following figures: In the six years from 1849 to 1854, inclusive, our total production of iron rails amounted to 336,930 tons, but in the same six years our imports of iron rails amounted to 1,227,310 tons. More than three and a half tons were imported for every ton that was made at home.

Professor Francis Bowen, of Harvard College, in his *Principles of Political Economy*, published in 1855, records in the following language some of the general effects of the tariff of 1846: "In 1850 and 1851 the average price of flour in our Atlantic seaports was about $5 a barrel, a price at which the farmers of the West can not afford to export it at all, except for the purpose of relieving a glutted market by a sacrifice. Meanwhile the sale of British manufactures in this country, to the great depression of our domestic industry, rapidly increased. Our imports of the manufactures of wool, cotton, and iron for the year ending in June, 1851, had become 43 per cent. and for that ending in June, 1853, 125 per cent. greater than they were the year before the alteration of the tariff. To pay for these extravagant importations we were obliged to sell our agricultural products at the reduced price just mentioned and to export an immense amount of California gold besides. This is not all. Within three years after this reduction of the tariff the price of the imported iron began to rise rapidly, and in 1852 and 1853 it was even higher than it had been before the ruin of the home manufacture."

Professor Bowen also states that "within three years after the effects of the new tariff began to be felt" 167 out of 304 blast furnaces in Pennsylvania were out of blast, being 55 per cent., "and the iron made by the remainder was 49 per cent. less than the quantity previously manufactured." "Within two years after the enactment of the new tariff" the product of the 200 establishments for the manufacture of wrought iron in Pennsylvania was reduced 33 per cent. Professor Bowen estimates that in the whole country "the new tariff threw out of employment 40,000 laborers" in the iron business alone, a large number of persons to be idle in this country in one industry half a century ago.

A leading feature of the tariff of 1846 was the general substitution of ad valorem for specific duties—a change utterly at war with the protective policy. When imports are entered at low prices duties are low and the home manufacturer loses the protection which he then most needs; when imports are entered at high prices duties are advanced and the home manufacturer is bountifully protected when protection is least needed. An ad valorem duty of 25 per cent. on foreign pig iron costing $8 per ton would protect the home manufacturer $2 per ton when he might be sorely pressed by foreign competition, but if the price of foreign pig iron should advance to $16 per ton the home manufacturer with the same ad valorem duty would receive $4 per ton protection when he did not need it, while an unnecessary burden would be placed upon the domestic consumer of foreign pig iron. And so with all other commodities which might be subject to ad valorem duties.

If ad valorem duties are continued long enough with imports at low prices there will be few home manufactures with which to compete when prices advance. Precisely this experience followed the passage of the tariff of 1846. British manufacturers threw their goods on our markets at extremely low prices, and, while the enemies of protection were pointing to these cheap goods as proof of the wisdom which had framed a purely revenue tariff, many of the manufacturing establishments of the country ceased to manufacture, men everywhere were thrown out of employment, and the brief prosperity which succeeded the passage of the tariff of 1842 quickly departed. Then, when domestic competition was no longer feared, because it was no longer hopeful or enterprising or powerful, the prices of foreign commodities were advanced and the foreign manufacturer reaped a bountiful harvest.

The average annual price of iron rails in this country fell from $53.88 per ton in 1849 to $45.63 in 1851. After 1851, the development of our iron rail industry having been thoroughly checked, the average price advanced as follows: 1852, $48.38; 1853, $77.25; 1854, $80.13; 1855, $62.88; 1856, $64.38; 1857, $64.25. In 1857 a great panic occurred, as the result of heavy importations of foreign goods and a further reduction of duties, the price of iron rails going down in the general crash.

The average annual price of bar iron in this country during the same period fell and rose and then fell again, as did the price of iron rails. It fell from $67.50 per ton in 1849 to $54.66 in 1851. Then, with most of our rolling mills either silent or working spasmodically, and with a thorough check to further rolling-mill development, the price began to rise. In 1852 it was $58.79; in 1853, $83.50; in 1854, $91.33; in 1855, $74.58; in 1856, $73.75; in 1857, $71.04.

In his third annual message, dated December 6, 1852, President Fillmore said: "The destruction of our manufactures leaves the foreigner without competition in our market, and he consequently *raises the price of the article sent here for sale, as is now seen in the increased cost of iron imported from England.*" In 1857, from sheer exhaustion, as the result of an experience of more than ten years with a tariff for revenue only, we began to buy less and less abroad and prices rapidly went down.

The New York *Tribune* for January 15, 1855, presented to its readers the following object lesson showing the painful consequences of the reduction of duties to a revenue basis in 1846. "Who is hungry? Go and see. You that are full-fed and know not what it is to be hungry—perhaps never saw a hungry man—go and see. Go and see a thousand men, women, boys, girls, old and young, black and white, of all nations but one—there are no Americans—crowding and jostling each other, almost fighting for a first chance—acting more like hungry wolves than human beings in a land of plenty. . . . Such a scene may be seen every day, from 11 till 2 o'clock, around the corner of Orange and Chatham streets, where Lindenmuller gives a dinner to the poor and soup and bread to others to carry to their miserable families.

... On Saturday we spent an hour there at the time of high tide. We have never seen anything like it before. On Friday upwards of a thousand people were fed with a plate of soup, a piece of bread, and a piece of meat on the premises, and in all upwards of sixteen hundred. On the same day 1,130 portions of soup were dealt out from Stewart's soup kitchen in the rear of the great marble palace store, corner of Reade street and Broadway. . . . At the rooms in Duane street for the relief of the poor of the sixth ward, on the same day, they gave food to 2,256. At the Five Points House of Industry, on the same day, . . . it is calculated that a thousand meals were given—say 700 different persons fed. Counting the number at the Old Bowery Mission at only half that number, we have, in the sixth ward, a total of over 6,000 persons fed by charity on Friday, January 12th. . . . Recollect, this is only one day in one ward."

The tariff of 1857, which was approved by President Pierce on March 3, 1857, reduced duties below the rates in the tariff of 1846, continuing the revenue policy of that act. The panic of 1857 followed. Upon many imported articles the tariff of 1846 imposed an ad valorem duty of 30 per cent., which the tariff of 1857 reduced to 24 per cent. The Boston *Sentinel* for October 24, 1885, gives the following picture of the effects of the tariff of 1857 upon the industries of Massachusetts.

"The industrial situation in 1857, and we might add all through President Buchanan's Administration, [from 1857 to 1861,] was most depressing. There was no certainty of employment for factory or machine-shop operatives. Wages were low and very uncertain. Half the time small manufacturers paid their help in orders on country stores, and the store men charged whatever they pleased. Jack-spinners, for instance, worked when they could get work for less than 80 cents a day, and we have full recollection that in the Fitchburg, Massachusetts, woolen mill they worked fourteen hours a day for $14 a month and board. They got paid once in every three months, and yet this was considered one of the best mills to work in in those days because it was steady and never was known to stop or suspend. In the large manufacturing cities, in Lowell, Lawrence, etc., there was positive want among the poorer operatives. In Lawrence, particularly, which was a new city and had a large number of new arrivals that had nothing laid away, there was a sad state of affairs. Real estate tumbled to a mere nothing. In some parts of the city it could scarcely be disposed of at any price. We have a vivid recollection of these and hundreds of other similar facts."

The experience of Massachusetts under the tariff of 1857 was shared by every other State in the Union. There was no prosperity anywhere. Judge Kelley says that the period from 1857 to the fall of 1861 was one of the darkest ever seen by the laboring people of America. The Judge adds: "In Philadelphia, when they wanted to build a street railroad, they advertised for two hundred and fifty hands at sixty cents a day, and more than five thousand offered, a majority of whom were skilled artisans who could find no other employment. In the neighborhood of one of the establishments, a rolling mill, the number of unemployed men was so great that the county authorities, to save its skilled workmen from open pauperism, determined to build a turnpike, and experienced hands from rolling mills were employed at breaking stone and road-making at fifty cents a day rather than become paupers."

So inadequate were the revenues from the tariff of 1857 that Mr. Buchanan was compelled near the close of his term to borrow money to save the public credit. The Morrill tariff act of March 2, 1861, therefore became a financial necessity of the Government as well as a means of rehabilitating the prostrated industries of the country.

No finer compliment has ever been paid to Hon. Justin S. Morrill, who is now (in 1897) in his 88th year and an active member of the United States Senate, than that which was conveyed to him in the following letter from the first of American political economists the day after the Morrill tariff bill passed the Senate and prior to its approval by President Buchanan:

*Dear Sir:* Accept my congratulations upon the happy termination of your tariff labours. You have now connected your name with what is destined, as I think, to prove the most important measure ever adopted by Congress. With great regard,

Yours Very Truly, HENRY C. CAREY.

PHILADELPHIA, February 27, 1861.

Various supplements to the tariff act of 1861 were enacted during the period of the civil war and immediately after its close, all of which continued the protective policy and some of which materially increased duties.

## CHAPTER XI.

### TARIFF LEGISLATION FROM 1870 TO 1897.

OUR personal knowledge of tariff legislation at Washington dates from the early months of 1870 and covers the intervening period of twenty-eight years. The Forty-first Congress was then in session, and a general revision of the various tariff laws of the war period was one of the important measures under consideration. Both branches of Congress were Republican. Mr. Blaine was the Speaker of the House of Representatives. On July 14, 1870, the Schenck tariff bill, which had been debated for almost six months, became a law, taking effect on January 1, 1871. One of its leading features was the levying of a duty of $28 per ton on steel rails, which duty subsequently built up our great steel rail industry. Another feature was the repeal of the income tax which had been imposed during the war. The whole scope and intention of the tariff act of 1870 were most friendly to American industries, and the consequences of this legislation were of immense value and of far-reaching importance. The tariff act of 1870 definitely fixed the revenue policy of the Republican party in time of peace on protectionist lines, and this tariff was a strong bulwark of defense for the industries of the country during the trying years following the panic of 1873. It was in force without material change for thirteen years, until 1883, when it was succeeded by the tariff act of that year, which was also a measure of protection.

General Robert C. Schenck's services to his country in

passing through the House the tariff act of 1870, against formidable opposition, entitle his name to rank in the list of its greatest benefactors. But for the protective features of the act of 1870, many of which were vigorously opposed by members of the House in General Schenck's own party, our leading mining and manufacturing industries would have been completely overwhelmed by foreign competition during the panic years from 1873 to 1879, and the hardships and privations of that dark period would have been increased beyond calculation. Nor could the country have bounded forward as it did in 1879 and 1880 if a less protective tariff than that of 1870 had been in force. General Schenck's courage and skill in passing this measure through the House have never been excelled in a legislative struggle.

There was important tariff legislation in the years 1871, 1872, and 1875. Congressional action in 1871 and 1872 was upon two bills, both aiming at a reduction of revenue, which had become excessive. The Republicans were in control of the House. Mr. Blaine was the Speaker. The first bill, to repeal the duties on tea and coffee, was introduced in the House by Samuel J. Randall, Democrat, of Pennsylvania, in 1871, and it passed that body without debate. In 1872, under the active leadership of Senator John Scott, Republican, of Pennsylvania, it passed the Senate, becoming a law on May 1, 1872, and taking effect on July 1st of the same year. The second bill was introduced in the House in 1872 by Mr. Dawes, chairman of the Committee on Ways and Means, and provided for a reduction of 10 per cent. on a large number of articles, many iron and steel articles being included. This bill passed both houses by large majorities and became a law on June 6, 1872, taking effect on August

1st. This legislation was a mistake, as it needlessly encouraged importations of foreign goods. An agitation in favor of its repeal resulted in the passage in 1875 of a bill containing a repealing provision, which became a law and took effect on March 3, 1875. This repealing provision was associated with other provisions affecting internal revenue taxes. By the passage of the act of March 3, 1875, virtually all duties on manufactured articles were restored to the rates fixed in the Schenck tariff of 1870. The duties on tea and coffee, which were repealed in 1872, have never since been restored, in whole or in part.

In 1876, the Democrats having control of the House of Representatives, and Mr. Kerr, of Indiana, an intense free trader, being the Speaker, Mr. Morrison, the chairman of the Committee on Ways and Means, introduced a complete tariff bill, which was not considered by the House and was never voted upon. The Wood tariff bill of 1878, the Democrats again having control of the House of Representatives, gave the manufacturers of the country great anxiety, but after a long discussion it was defeated upon the motion of General Butler to strike out the enacting clause, the vote being 134 yeas to 121 nays, 19 Democrats voting to strike out. Mr. Randall, a sound protectionist, although a Democrat, was the Speaker of the House at this time, having in 1876 succeeded Mr. Kerr, who died in that year.

A determined effort to reduce the steel rail duty to $10 per ton was made in 1880, through the Covert bill, but this measure was beaten in the Committee on Ways and Means, after a spirited hearing by the committee of the domestic manufacturers of steel rails and of representatives of a few railroad companies which asked for the proposed reduction.

The defeat of the bill in the committee turned upon one vote, a motion to lay it on the table receiving seven affirmative and six negative votes. This decisive action was taken on March 2, 1880. That was a critical time for our steel rail industry. At the same session of the committee a bill introduced by Mr. Morrison, providing that, in certain specified schedules of the existing tariff, no duty should be levied in excess of 50 per cent. of the foreign value of the article imported, was also laid on the table by the same vote.

The defeat of the Covert bill to reduce the duty on steel rails to $10 per ton was secured in large part by the intelligent and active exertions of Judge William D. Kelley, of Pennsylvania, a member of the Committee on Ways and Means, whose devotion to the protective policy during his long service of almost thirty years in the House of Representatives, from 1861 to 1890, never flagged for one moment. His advocacy of this policy was never apologetic and was always aggressive. His courage saved the day in more than one crisis when protection was endangered fully as much by the attitude of some of its friends as by the attacks of its outspoken enemies. He stands at the head of all the Congressional advocates of protection in this generation. He was a hard student, an accomplished rhetorician, and a born orator. His "Reasons for Abandoning the Theory of Free Trade," prefixed to a volume of his *Speeches, Addresses, and Letters*, should be read by every student of political economy.

The tariff act of 1883 was a measure of protection, framed by a Republican Congress on the lines of the Schenck bill, but lacking in symmetry and bearing on almost every page marks of the haste of a committee of conference. The act followed in part the suggestions of a Tariff Commission which had been authorized by Congress in 1882 and which had been appointed by President Arthur. The commission prepared a complete tariff bill. The act of 1883 was the work chiefly of the Senate Committee on Finance and of a committee of conference. It would have been better if the bill of the Tariff Commission had been accepted without material amendment. Mr. Keifer was the Speaker of the House at this time and Judge Kelley was the chairman of the Committee on Ways and Means.

John L. Hayes, of Boston, secretary of the National Association of Wool Manufacturers, was the president of the Tariff Commission. His great work in life was his earnest advocacy of the protective policy. He was not excelled in the earnestness and zeal with which he advocated this policy; in the fullness of his knowledge of his subject he had few equals. He was an accomplished scholar and a writer of the purest and strongest English of this age of good English writing. Nowhere can we find greater ease, simplicity, grace, and force of expression, clearer presentation of facts, or more orderly and logical arrangement of details than in his numerous addresses, essays, and other publications. He also possessed a fine poetic sense, which is visible in many of his voluminous prose writings, but is found in its most perfect manifestation in that wonderful work produced during his last illness—his translation of mediæval Latin hymns.

Soon after the passage of the tariff act of 1883 the Democrats, again having a majority in the House, began an agitation for its repeal. Mr. Carlisle was the Speaker in 1884 when Mr. Morrison, who was again the chairman of the Committee on Ways and Means, introduced in the House his twenty-per-cent. "horizontal reduction" tariff bill, which led to a long debate, resulting in the defeat of the bill upon the motion of Mr. Converse, Democrat, to strike out the enacting clause, Mr. Randall and 39 other Democrats voting with Mr. Converse. The House was Democratic by a large majority. The vote was 159 to strike out and 155 to sustain the bill.

In November of the same year Mr. Cleveland was elected to the Presidency. In his first annual message to Congress, in December, 1885, Mr. Cleveland recommended a general reduction of duties. Mr. Carlisle was again Speaker and Mr. Morrison was again at the head of the Committee on Ways and Means. Early in 1886 Mr. Morrison introduced another bill to revise and reduce the tariff. This bill was also defeated, the House, which was again Democratic by a large majority, refusing even to consider it, the vote being 140 yeas to 157 nays, Mr. Randall and 34 other Democrats voting to kill the bill. For this vote Mr. Cleveland never forgave Mr. Randall.

In his next annual message, submitted in December, 1886, Mr. Cleveland again recommended a reduction of duties, and in the same month Mr. Morrison brought forward his tariff bill of the preceding session, but the House again refused to consider it, the vote being 149 yeas to 154 nays, Mr. Randall and 25 other Democrats voting in the negative. That was the virtual end of tariff agitation in that Congress.

But Mr. Cleveland was determined to have his own way, and in his annual message in December, 1887, he again recommended a reduction of duties. This message marked a more radical advance by Mr. Cleveland toward free trade than any of his previous utterances on the tariff question, and it alarmed the country. In January, 1888, Mr. Mills, of Texas, became the chairman of the new Committee on

Ways and Means, the House again being Democratic, and Mr. Carlisle again being Speaker. On March 1st Mr. Mills submitted to the committee his now famous tariff bill, which proposed a general reduction of duties. Before a vote upon its merits had been taken in the House Mr. Cleveland was nominated at St. Louis, in June, for a second term upon a platform specifically indorsing his tariff views. In the same month General Harrison was nominated at Chicago for the Presidency upon a platform in which the Mills bill was denounced by name. On July 21st the Mills bill passed the House by a vote of 162 yeas to 149 nays. Only four Democrats voted against it. Mr. Randall would have also voted against the bill if he had not been too ill to be in his seat.

Not a great scholar, nor a great orator, nor a great writer, Samuel J. Randall was nevertheless a man of sterling common sense, quick perceptions, great courage, broad views, and extraordinary capacity for work. He had the courage of Andrew Jackson and the kindness of heart of Abraham Lincoln. He was born for public affairs and he was a born leader of men. Like his great townsman, Judge Kelley, he was a thorough American in all his instincts and aspirations. His ardent patriotism made him a strong protectionist all his days, although the Democratic party to which he belonged has in late years widely differed with him on economic questions, and with Madison and others who founded it. His services to the industries of his country have been invaluable. On more than one critical occasion he stood in the breach and prevented by his own determined will the infliction of serious injury to those industries from that wing of his party which did not sympathize with his protectionist convictions.

In behalf of the Republican majority in the Senate Senator Allison, chairman of a sub-committee of the Committee on Finance, submitted on October 3, 1888, a substitute for the Mills bill. The substitute was a thoroughly protective measure. Both bills were fully discussed in the Senate and on the stump and in the newspapers during the remainder of the Presidential campaign. The Senate substitute passed that body on January 22, 1889, by a vote of 32 yeas to 30 nays. It was never considered by the House. The Mills bill was, however, dead. In the meantime, in November, 1888, Mr. Cleveland had been defeated for the Presidency by a close vote, the principal issue being the tariff question as it was presented in the two bills referred to. At the same election the Republicans succeeded to the control of the House of Representatives.

As a logical sequence of the Republican success in 1888 the House of Representatives, when it met in December, 1889, undertook the revision of the tariff of 1883 on the lines of the Senate substitute for the Mills bill. This revision subsequently became a law and is known as the McKinley tariff, William McKinley being the chairman of the Committee on Ways and Means which framed the bill. Mr. Reed was the Speaker. The McKinley tariff bill passed the House on May 21, 1890, by a vote of 164 yeas to 142 nays. It passed the Senate on September 10th by a vote of 40 yeas to 29 nays, and after passing through a committee of conference it became a law on October 1st, taking effect on October 6th. The Senate had made many changes in the House bill, some of these changes materially reducing duties, but in the conference committee most of the original House rates were restored. A prominent feature of the new tariff was the insertion of an adequately protective duty on tinplates, which at once gave a great impetus to the establishment of a tinplate industry in our country—an industry which had not previously had an existence on American soil, except as an experiment which had failed through the pressure of foreign competition.

An important service was rendered by Senator Quay, of Pennsylvania, in connection with the McKinley tariff bill. The bill was jeopardized in the Senate by the Federal Elections bill, the so-called "Force bill," which many Republican Senators were determined to pass and which Democratic Senators, who were in the minority, were determined to defeat by obstructive tactics, or, in other words, by talking the bill to death. If this scheme of the Democrats had been carried out they would not only have succeeded in defeating the "Force bill" but they would also have prevented the passage of the McKinley tariff bill through the Senate, as the time consumed in killing the "Force bill" would have prevented the consideration of the McKinley bill. Senator Quay had the skill and adroitness to rescue the McKinley bill from this serious dilemma by securing the adoption of an order of business which gave it the right of way over the "Force bill." Thenceforward the bill had plain sailing.

At the Congressional elections in 1890 which immediately followed the enactment of the McKinley tariff the Republican party was defeated, and at the Presidential and Congressional elections in 1892 it was again defeated. Mr. Cleveland, now a virtual free trader, was again elected to the Presidency. For the first time in almost forty years the Presidency and both branches of Congress passed into the hands of the Democratic party. This revolution, which was the result in large part of widespread discontent with existing social conditions, was of so sweeping a character and threatened such radical changes in tariff and financial legislation that thoughtful business men, including many who had supported the successful party, at once became alarmed. A tightening of the money market soon followed and many failures occurred. Stocks rapidly declined. Confidence in the stability of the currency was shaken by heavy gold shipments. On May 3, 1893, Wall street was the scene of intense excitement, and on that day another great financial panic had its beginning. This panic, with its attendant consequences and accompanying disturbances, rested like a pall upon the industries of the country until the summer of 1897.

President Cleveland convened Congress in special session on the 7th of August, 1893, to consider the financial crisis, which he attributed to an unwise financial policy embodied in unwise laws. Both houses of Congress met on the day mentioned, and on the 1st of November the President signed the Voorhees bill repealing the silver-purchase provision of the Sherman act of 1890. It is enough to say of this legislation, which occupied almost three months of time, that it did not accomplish the results that had been claimed for it. The people were not "relieved through legislation," to quote the President's language, "from present and impending danger and distress." The depression continued and increased in severity.

While the repeal of the Sherman act was under consideration a new tariff bill was in course of preparation by the Committee on Ways and Means, in compliance with the President's wishes, Mr. Wilson being chairman of the committee. Mr. Crisp was the Speaker. When Congress met in regular session in December the so-called Wilson tariff bill was at once perfected, and on the 19th of December it was reported to the House. It passed that body on the 1st of February, 1894. On the 3d of July a substitute for the Wilson bill, which embodied much more favorable consideration of American interests and less regard for foreign interests, passed the Senate. The two bills were considered for several weeks in a conference committee, and on August 13th the whole subject was finally disposed of by the passage through the House of the Senate bill. It did not receive the President's approval, but it became a law on August 28, 1894, through the failure of the President to interpose a veto.

Senator Quay's part in securing the defeat of the original Wilson tariff bill in 1894 and the substitution of higher rates of duty for hundreds of its practically free trade provisions can not be overlooked by the impartial historian. It was of inestimable value to the country. The Senator did not need to convince Senator Gorman and four or five other Democratic Senators of the destructive character of the Wilson bill, but it was vitally necessary that about thirty other Democratic Senators should be convinced that, if they did not vote to give at least partial protection to the industries which had been so seriously threatened by the Wilson bill, that bill could never become a law; with the assistance of other Republicans he would deal with it as the Democrats had proposed to deal with the "Force bill." This threat, which was partly carried out by the delivery of the Senator's obstructive speech, occupying twelve days in April, May, and June, 1894, had the effect that was desired. The tariff bill which became a law was not the original Wilson bill at all. Many of its worst features were eliminated.

That the difference between the Wilson bill as it passed the House and the Senate substitute may be clearly understood a few of the provisions of the metal schedule of the two bills may be mentioned. The Wilson bill placed coal and iron ore in the free list; the Senate bill imposed a duty of 40 cents per ton on both articles. The Wilson bill placed a duty of 20 per cent. on pig iron, equivalent to a specific duty of from $1.50 to $2 per ton; the Senate bill imposed a duty of $4 per ton, or fully twice as much as the Wilson bill. The Wilson bill placed a duty of 20 per cent. on steel rails, equivalent to a specific duty of from $3.25 to $3.50 per ton; the Senate bill imposed a duty of $7.84 per ton, or more than twice as much as the Wilson bill. The Wilson bill placed a duty of 30 per cent. upon structural shapes of iron or steel, equivalent to a specific duty of about $6 per ton; the Senate bill imposed a duty of $13.44 per ton, or more than twice as much as the Wilson bill. Many other radical changes in the metal schedule of the Wilson bill which were made by the Senate and forced upon the House might be added to the above. Some of the other schedules of the Wilson bill did not fare so well in the hands of the Senate as the metal schedule. The cotton schedule fared fully as well. But all the schedules were made more protective by the Senate than they were in the original Wilson bill, which proposed a great stride toward free trade.

Nevertheless the amended Wilson tariff bill gave a severe blow to the industries of the country. One of its worst features was the placing of wool in the free list, and another was the serious reduction in the duties on woolen goods. Notwithstanding a partial revival of confidence and of business activity following the passage of the amended Wilson bill the country did not approve of that act of legislation. The Congressional elections of 1894 were carried by the Republicans, and in 1896 the Presidency itself was captured by them, the House of Representatives remaining Republican by a large majority. In the elections of 1894 and 1896 the Wilson tariff was a leading issue. At both elections the people voted for a restoration of the protective policy.

With the election of William McKinley to the Presidency in November, 1896, public opinion at once demanded the repeal of the Wilson tariff at the earliest possible moment. On March 4, 1897, President McKinley was inaugurated, and on the 6th he issued a proclamation convening the Fifty-fifth Congress in special session on the 15th. On the day last mentioned Congress met, and on the same day Mr. Reed was again elected Speaker of the House and he at once appointed the Committee on Ways and Means, with Mr. Dingley, of Maine, as chairman. On the same day Mr. Dingley reported a complete tariff bill to the House, which bill had been in preparation by the Republican members of the committee since Congress met in regular session in the preceding December, Mr. Dingley then being its chairman. On the 31st this bill passed the House by a vote of 205 yeas to 122 nays. On April 1st it was received by the Senate and was at once referred to the Committee on Finance, which committee reported it back to the Senate on May 4th, with a large number of proposed amendments. On July 7th the bill passed the Senate, with 871 actual amendments, by a vote of 38 yeas to 28 nays, and it was at once referred to a committee of conference. On July 19th it was reported back to the House from this committee, and on the 20th the report of the conference committee was adopted by that body by a vote of 186 yeas to 115 nays. On the 24th the report was adopted by the Senate by a vote of 40 yeas to 30 nays. The bill was at once signed by the President and became a law, displacing entirely the Wilson tariff. It went into effect the same day.

It will be observed by the reader who has followed these reminiscences that the protective policy has often been in peril since 1870. We believe that it now rests on a firmer foundation of popular regard than ever before in our history. There will be no general revision of the tariff during the remainder of this century, and during this time the country will have comparative peace from tariff agitation.

## CHAPTER XII.

### ALEXANDER HAMILTON.

SATURDAY, December 5, 1891, was the hundredth anniversary of the transmission to the Second Congress of the United States by Alexander Hamilton, Secretary of the Treasury, of his celebrated "Report on the Subject of Manufactures," which embodies the earliest elaborate plea in behalf of our protective policy that our protectionist literature affords. A copy of this able and unanswerable report, edited by Mathew Carey, and printed in Philadelphia in 1827, and filling 71 pages of close type, is before us. Among the many excellent arguments in behalf of protection which it contains we take at random one strong sentence: "When all the different kinds of industry obtain in a community each individual can find his proper element and can call into activity the whole vigor of his nature."

The Second Congress met in Philadelphia in December, 1791. From the date of Hamilton's report until the present time Philadelphia has been the foremost city in the Union in advocating and defending the protective policy which he so clearly and so ably outlined and so successfully commended to his countrymen. The new government had started in 1789 with a protective tariff, but Hamilton's great report assured the ascendancy of the protective policy in our national legislation until 1816, when we began to depart from it, with evil consequences which Henry Clay has so graphically described.

It is a fact worthy of notice that Hamilton advocated in his report the policy of granting government bounties to aid in the establishment of new industries in our country, and that his recommendation was never carried into effect until exactly one hundred years after it was made, when, under the tariff of 1890, we began to pay a bounty for the production of sugar. This bounty provision was subsequently repealed in the tariff act of 1894 and it has not since been reenacted. It was a great mistake. But the policy which was clearly a mistake in 1890 might have proved to be an eminently wise policy in 1791 if it had been carried into effect.

In Mathew Carey's preface to the edition of Hamilton's report which we have before us he says: "I hope we shall live to see the day—if we do not assuredly our children will—when medals will be struck and monuments erected to the memory of Alexander Hamilton!" But no medals have been struck and no monuments have been erected in memory of this father of the American policy of protection to home industry, except the small and timeworn shaft erected by relatives over his grave in Trinity churchyard in New York. But Hamilton's memory may yet be suitably honored.

In a letter which we have received from Hon. John Dalzell, a distinguished Representative in Congress from Pennsylvania, who has been a member of the Ways and Means Committee since 1891, that gentleman says of Hamilton: "His tariff argument has never been added to. Every tariff speech in our history simply repeats the ideas that he stated in the first instance. We have never done him justice. Jefferson is lauded while Hamilton is neglected. He ought to stand a colossal figure in bronze or marble in front of the Treasury."

# CHAPTER XIII.

### TARIFF CONVENTIONS IN THE OLDEN TIME.

On Monday, July 30, 1827, a meeting of delegates from the States of Connecticut, Delaware, Kentucky, Maryland, Massachusetts, New York, New Hampshire, New Jersey, Ohio, Pennsylvania, Rhode Island, Vermont, and Virginia convened at the capitol building at Harrisburg, Pennsylvania, in pursuance of a call issued on the 14th of May preceding by the Pennsylvania Society for the Promotion of Manufactures and the Mechanic Arts. The convention was composed of one hundred delegates. The names of some of the delegates are among the most prominent in our history. Connecticut sent Gideon Welles; Massachusetts, Abbott Lawrence; New York, Francis Granger; New Hampshire, Ezekiel Webster; Ohio, Thomas Ewing; Pennsylvania, Charles J. Ingersoll, Mathew Carey, and Walter Forward; Rhode Island, Ashur Robbins; and Vermont, Rollin C. Mallary. The New York delegation was numerically the strongest, embracing eighteen members, and that of Pennsylvania was the next in numerical strength, embracing fifteen members. Joseph Ritner, afterwards Governor of Pennsylvania, was the president of the convention. The convention was in session four days, and as one result of its labors it adopted a brief but practical address to Congress in favor of the policy of protection to the then infant manufactures of the country. It was prepared by a committee of which Mr. Ingersoll was chairman. An address to the country was also adopted, which was prepared mainly by Hezekiah Niles, of Maryland. These addresses contributed greatly to the passage of the eminently wise tariff act of 1828.

On Wednesday, October 26, 1831, a general convention of the friends of home industry assembled at New York, which remained in session a whole week. This also was a convention of delegates. The following States were represented: Maine, New Hampshire, Vermont, Massachusetts, Rhode Island, Connecticut, New York, New Jersey, Pennsylvania, Delaware, Maryland, Virginia, and Ohio, and the District of Columbia. Over five hundred delegates were in attendance. In the list of members are the names of many leading business men and historical personages of that time. Near the top of the list we meet the name of Samuel Garfield, of New Hampshire. The best families in New England were represented by such names as Alexander H. Everett, Abbott Lawrence, William Appleton, and Samuel Hoar, of Massachusetts; Zachariah Allen, James F. Simmons, Richard Anthony, and Nathan F. Dixon, of Rhode Island; and many others of equal eminence. James Tallmadge, Peter R. Livingston, Benjamin B. Howell, Asabel Seward, Gurdon Corning, and Charles H. Morrell were among the hundred representatives from New York; David Reeves and Thomas Rodgers were two of the fifty delegates from New Jersey; and S. V. Merrick, Mathew Carey, A. M. Jones, Ellis Lewis, John J. Borie, James M. Haldeman, Jonathan Roberts, J. P. Wetherill, William Wilkins, Walter Forward, and Benjamin Reeves were among the hundred delegates from Pennsylvania. John P. Kennedy was one of many delegates from Maryland. William Wilkins, of Pennsylvania, was the president of the convention, and Hezekiah Niles, of Maryland, was the principal secretary. The convention was called to take notice of the proceedings of a convention of free traders held at Philadelphia in September and October of the same year, and to reply to a memorial to Congress which it had adopted. The memorial of this free trade convention was written by Albert Gallatin, who had been Secretary of the Treasury under Jefferson and Madison and had held other positions of responsibility and honor. It remonstrated with a great deal of logical force and with no little sophistry against the continuance of the protective tariff of 1828.

The New York convention appointed committees to report on the leading industries of the country, showing the beneficial effects upon each of them of the protective policy as it had been embodied in the tariff acts of 1824 and 1828. These committees submitted very interesting reports, some of which were prepared with great care. Two other committees were appointed to prepare respectively a memorial to Congress and an address to the country. The memorial, which was written by Alexander H. Everett, was a complete answer to Mr. Gallatin's assumptions, and was in all respects a profound and masterly presentation of the wisdom of protection. But political, or rather sectional, considerations were too powerful at this time for the friends of home industry, and in February, 1833, Mr. Clay introduced his compromise tariff bill, which gave away all that had been gained in the tariffs of 1824 and 1828. It was not until 1842 that the country again returned to the protective policy, which was in force only until 1846.

The enactment of the revenue tariff of 1846 was attended with such disastrous consequences to the iron trade of the whole country that vigorous protests against its longer continuance were inevitable. A convention of dissatisfied iron manufacturers, composed of about 160 delegates from New York, New Jersey, Pennsylvania, Ohio, Kentucky, Virginia, and Illinois, met "in the new court-house" at Pittsburgh, on Wednesday, November 21, 1849, and continued in session for three days. The convention was presided over by Hon. James Rodgers, of Ohio. Among the prominent persons who were present and participated in the proceedings were Hon. Charles Shaler and Hon. Andrew Stewart, but the convention was almost wholly composed of practical iron manufacturers. Resolutions were adopted which declared that the tariff of 1846 had proved to be inadequate as a protection against foreign competition in the manufacture of iron and steel, and protesting against its general ad valorem character. The resolutions also bore testimony to the widespread depression which then existed in the agricultural industry of the country, which, it was declared, was largely dependent for its prosperity upon the iron industry and other manufacturing industries. Congress was called upon to grant relief by revising the tariff in the interest of home industry. A special committee was appointed to prepare a suitable memorial to Congress. The proceedings of the convention were published in the Pittsburgh *Gazette*.

On December 6, 1849, a call was issued by a number of iron manufacturers for a convention to meet at Philadelphia on December 20th, "to appeal to Congress, without distinction of party, for the preservation of a great American interest." A numerously attended convention, composed chiefly of Pennsylvania iron manufacturers, met in the chamber of the Board of Trade on the day mentioned. Thomas Chambers, of the Montour Iron Works, was chosen chairman of the convention. The proceedings of this convention have been preserved in book form, and they show that the men who participated in its deliberations were not only greatly in earnest but that they were also men of ability and force. A remarkably able memorial to Congress, written by Stephen Colwell, was adopted. A report on the statistics of the iron trade at home and abroad was presented by Charles E. Smith, which displayed great research in a field which at that time had been but little explored. Mr. Smith subsequently prepared a detailed statement of the condition of the iron industry of Pennsylvania, which was completed on June 1, 1850, and is bound up with the proceedings of the convention. This statement showed by name the furnaces and other iron enterprises in the State which had been wrecked by the tariff of 1846. It was the result of a personal "tour through the State."

Bound up with the proceedings also is a letter addressed on December 26, 1849, to the New York *Journal of Commerce* by Cooper & Hewitt, setting forth with great ability the resources of the country for the production of iron and the injury that had been inflicted upon this industry by the tariff of 1846. Mr. Abram S. Hewitt was a delegate to the convention and a member of the committee on resolutions. There was also bound up with the proceedings a paper by Henry C. Carey on "The Harmony of Interests," in which the relation of the iron industry to other industries was thoroughly discussed.

The resolutions adopted by the convention stated that " a crisis has arisen in the iron business which calls for the immediate revision of the revenue laws," and called upon Congress to grant relief by increasing duties. A " general committee," to further the objects of the convention, was appointed. It does not appear, however, that either this convention or the one held at Pittsburgh a few weeks previously made any serious impression upon Congress. The tariff of 1846 was not disturbed.

A national tariff convention met at the Cooper Institute, New York, on Tuesday, November 29, 1881, and continued in session during the following day. This convention was called by a committee of active protectionists, in response to a widespread sentiment in favor of a closer union of the protectionists of the whole country. The call fixed the number of delegates to the convention at six hundred, allotted as equitably as possible among the different trades and industries, and nearly the whole number were present at the meeting of the convention. Peter Cooper, who was then in his 91st year, was one of the delegates and made a short address. Hon. George B. Loring, United States Commissioner of Agriculture, was the temporary chairman of the convention, and Hon. Warner Miller, United States Senator from New York, was the permanent chairman. Among the vice presidents were Hon. B. F. Jones, of Pittsburgh, and Hon. Columbus Delano, of Ohio. Both the presiding officers delivered elaborate addresses upon taking the chair. A letter was read from Hon. James G. Blaine, Secretary of State, which was written in Mr. Blaine's characteristically happy style, and in which he first hinted at the reciprocity policy that he afterwards succeeded in engrafting upon the tariff legislation of 1890.

Addresses were delivered by Hon. William McKinley, of Ohio; Hon. William D. Kelley, Joseph Wharton, and James Dobson, of Philadelphia; John H. Ricketson and John

Jarrett, of Pittsburgh; Wellington Smith and Theodore C. Bates, of Massachusetts; Hon. J. B. Grinnell, of Iowa; Hon. J. Hart Brewer, of New Jersey; John Roach, of New York; Giles B. Stebbins, of Michigan; Hon. W. S. Shallenberger, of Pennsylvania; Hon. Edward T. Johnson, of Indiana; Col. John Scriven, of Georgia, and many others. Judge Kelley's address dealt chiefly with our internal revenue system and its relation to the industries of the country. He favored the total abolition of internal taxes at the earliest day possible. Mr. Wharton's address was mainly a plea in favor of the policy of revising the tariff by a commission of experts, to be authorized by Congress and appointed by the President. Mr. Grinnell, who was for many years a Representative in Congress from Iowa, also supported the project of a tariff commission. In the introduction to his address he stated that he had at home a paper (we presume he meant a letter) which contained the "commission" that Horace Greeley once gave to him—"Young man, go West." Mr. Jarrett, who was at the time the president of the Amalgamated Association of Iron and Steel Workers, spoke for the workingmen of the country, explaining their interest in the cause of protection to home industry. Mr. Roach's address was devoted to the necessity of extending our foreign commerce, and he was followed upon the same theme by Mr. Johnson. In all forty-six addresses were delivered before the convention and five papers were read. Mr. A. H. Jones, of Philadelphia, read a valuable paper concerning the chemical industry.

A committee on an address and resolutions which should embody the views of the convention was appointed, and of this committee Cyrus Elder, of Johnstown, Pennsylvania, was chairman. The committee presented an exhaustive report, written by Mr. Elder, which was adopted. One of its leading features was a strong indorsement of the suggestion that the tariff should be revised by a commission. A committee was appointed to lay this report before both branches of Congress, which was afterwards done.

To the influence exerted by this convention may be credited the passage during the succeeding session of Congress of an act providing for the creation of a Tariff Commission, which was appointed by President Arthur in 1882, and which subsequently, during the same year, made a report to Congress, accompanied by a draft of a tariff bill. The proceedings of the convention were published in book form. The volume comprises one of the most valuable compilations of protective tariff literature to be found anywhere.

The conventions of 1827, 1831, and 1849 were composed of representatives of all the political parties that were in existence when they were held, and in all of these conventions there were no more earnest advocates of the protective policy than the Democratic delegates who participated in their deliberations. But it is noticeable that in the convention of 1881 there were very few Democrats, nearly all of the delegates being Republicans.

The American Iron Association was organized at Philadelphia on March 6, 1855. The object of this Association was the promotion of the mutual interests of American iron manufacturers, trade information and statistics being of first importance. Hon. George N. Eckert, of Reading, Pennsylvania, was chosen president; Gen. James Irvin and John H. Towne, vice presidents; Charles E. Smith, treasurer; and J. P. Lesley, secretary. The office of the Association was established at Philadelphia. The Association thus organized continued in active existence until 1859, having a life of four years. On November 16, 1864, the American Iron and Steel Association was organized at Philadelphia, and it has continued in active existence ever since, with its office also in Philadelphia. A leading object in establishing this Association was the promotion of the tariff interests of the whole American iron trade, but another leading object was the promotion of the protective policy for the benefit of all the industries of the country. It is the oldest tariff organization in the United States. It has held many public meetings for the consideration of tariff questions, but further reference in these pages to these meetings or to any of the work of the Association is not necessary. Its first officers were as follows: President, Captain E. B. Ward, of Detroit, Michigan; vice presidents, Samuel J. Reeves, Abram S. Hewitt, James M. Cooper, Charles S. Wood, and Joseph H. Scranton; treasurer, Charles Wheeler; and secretary, Robert H. Lamborn. Mr. Hewitt has remained a vice president ever since. It is, however, but just to say of this gentleman that he has not always approved of the tariff policy of the Association.

A convention of the iron manufacturers of Maryland was held in 1849 to protest against the tariff of 1846, and a report upon the depressed condition of the iron industries of that State was adopted, but further particulars of this convention are not accessible.

# CHAPTER XIV.

#### WHY THE SOUTHERN CONFEDERACY FAILED.

THE following provision is contained in the Constitution of the Confederate States of America, which was adopted at Montgomery, Alabama, on March 11, 1861. It will be seen that it prohibits the levying of protective duties.

"SEC. 8. Congress shall have power to lay and collect taxes, duties, imposts, and excises for revenue necessary to pay the debts, provide for the common defense, and carry on the government of the Confederate States. But no bounties shall be granted from the treasury nor shall any duties or taxes on importations from foreign nations be laid to promote or foster any branch of industry."

That the South seceded partly that it might establish free trade is frankly confessed by a distinguished native of South Carolina. In the course of an open letter to the chairman of the executive committee of the Free Trade Association of South Carolina, written on the 23d of April, 1886, the Hon. George D. Tillman, who served as a private in the Confederate army from early in 1862 to the close of the war and was subsequently a Democratic member of Congress, said: "Shall we of the Palmetto State always be self-idolatrous Bourbons, never forgetting, never learning, anything? Was it not our intemperate zeal for free trade that led to nullification, and was it not as much to enjoy free trade as to protect slavery that South Carolina seceded in 1860?"

In a leading editorial the New Orleans *Daily City Item*

discussed a few years ago the economic causes which contributed to the failure of the Southern Confederacy. It said: "With the South was courage, conviction, and unparalleled strategic ability in the field. There was a limited stock of mechanical supplies on hand. There was the right to sell in the dearest and buy in the cheapest markets of the world. So long as these supplies continued and this trade was free the Confederacy could arm and equip its armies and even import comforts and luxuries. Without shipping or sailors, or general commercial credits abroad, free trade soon ceased to be a sufficient reliance. As there were no manufactures adequate to supply the rapid consumption of goods imported before the war the privations of a highly civilized people were very grievous, while the suffering of the soldiers in camp or on the march was an element of depression and positive weakness. In this positive deficiency the occasional arrival of a blockade runner or capture of Yankee stores was an insufficient compensation. The disparity in resources told like the avoirdupois of the slugger against the pluck and science of the light weight. While such was the destitution of the South the condition of the North was never better." It was better, continued the *City Item*, because the North had developed its manufactures.

A similar Southern tribute to the excellence of our protective policy, and to its influence in blighting the hopes of the friends of the Southern Confederacy, was expressed a few years ago by General Richard Taylor, of Louisiana, a Confederate officer of distinction, in a review of the war which was expected to establish free trade as a means of prosperity in the South. General Taylor says: "We made two great mistakes. Had we avoided them we should have conquered you. The first was that we did not substantially destroy the protective features of the tariff in the winter session of 1857-8 by an act which provided a rapid sliding scale to free trade. As a Democratic measure we could have passed such a law and held it tight on you till it closed the furnaces, workshops, woolen and cotton mills, and steel and bar iron works of the whole North and West, and scattered your workmen over the prairies and Territories. When the war was ready for you you would not have been ready for the war. You could not have armed and equipped and put in the field a large army nor built a navy. You would have been without supplies, machinery, and workmen, and you would have been without money and credit. Our second mistake was in withdrawing our Senators and Representatives from your Congress. . . How we blundered in these two respects I can not understand, except upon the hypothesis of an overruling Providence." As we have previously shown, the tariff that was in force just before the war was not a protective measure, but manufactures had been developed in the North from the foundation of the Government, while in the South they had been neglected.

We are glad to add to the above that the South is now realizing in its increased attention to its native resources and to manufacturing enterprises many of the benefits of our protective policy. In the near future it is destined to enjoy still more of the blessings which follow a diversification of industrial pursuits.

# CHAPTER XV.

### PROTECTION IS NOT MONOPOLY.

It is a standing argument with those who oppose a protective tariff that it creates and fosters monopolies. A monopoly is defined by Webster to be "the sole power of dealing in any species of goods, or of dealing with a country or market, obtained either by engrossing the articles in market by purchase or by a license from government; sole permission and power to deal; exclusive command or possession."

Monopolies are not necessarily evils, and a great deal of the indiscriminate denunciation they receive is unmerited. The United States Government enjoys a monopoly of carrying the mails, but it will not be contended that this service would be better performed if it were in the hands of private individuals or competing companies. The Pennsylvania Railroad Company enjoys a monopoly of transporting freight and passengers through Pennsylvania between Philadelphia and Pittsburgh and intermediate points, but it does its work well, and no person will contend that the State of Pennsylvania and the country at large would be as far advanced as they are if the charter of the company had never been granted. Every railroad and other company which is chartered with special privileges is a monopoly, and most companies so chartered have promoted the public welfare, even when they have conspicuously promoted their own interests. Every street railway is by force of circumstances a monopoly, and so is every company that carries freight and passengers across a river; so is every turnpike company. Pullman's Palace Car Company is a monopoly on most of our railroads, and whether its service be good or bad all of us patronize it when we go away from home because we can not help ourselves. The Adams Express Company is a monopoly. The Western Union Telegraph Company is a monopoly which has virtually overcome all opposition and now charges the public what it pleases for the service it renders. The owners of our anthracite coal fields are monopolists, because they own the only anthracite coal fields of consequence in the country. But not one of these monopolies has been created by the tariff legislation of Congress.

There are giant monopolies in this country which conspicuously serve personal and selfish interests. The Standard Oil Company is an example of this class. It controls the great petroleum industry of the country and apparently aims to own it all. Tariff legislation neither created nor maintains it. But this monopoly has greatly cheapened the price of petroleum to all consumers.

We have mentioned monopolies which are great public blessings and other monopolies which serve the public but which draw largely upon its patience and often offend its sense of justice. There are other monopolies which ought not to exist. But none of these are the monopolies to which the opponents of our protective policy refer.

What monopolies has protection created, and where are they to be found? All the leading productive industries of the country are more or less protected by tariff legislation against foreign competition; our agricultural, mining, and manufacturing industries are so protected. Which one of these industries nurses a monopoly? Which branch of them is in the exclusive possession of any set of men? Our patent laws recognize the principle of exclusive ownership in an invention, but our protective policy grants exclusive privileges to none. Protection has never created or maintained even one monopoly in this country. On the contrary, the very intention of protection is to encourage enterprise and investments by many persons, so that industries may be developed by many hands and competition created. All this is the exact opposite of monopoly.

Combinations of producers to restrict production or to raise prices, which may or may not be justifiable, and which are of the essence of monopoly, are no more a consequence of protection than are combinations among workingmen to raise wages. Combinations of producers have been as common in free trade England as in our own country. They are a product of human nature and not of any economic policy. Nor has the tariff had anything to do with our wheat rings, pork rings, lard rings, and the whisky ring. The tariff is not responsible for any of them. Nor is it responsible for railroad pools or for any other combinations of mutual interests.

There has been one monopoly which was created and long maintained by American tariff legislation, but that legislation was not adopted as a part of our protective policy, nor was the monopoly referred to to be found in the United States. The monopoly we have in mind was the manufacture of tinplates for sale in the United States, and it was to be found in Great Britain. It was maintained down to 1890 by the persistent refusal of the American Congress to impose a protective duty which would enable us to make our own tinplates, which, as everybody knows, are almost entirely composed of iron or steel. As a result of this refusal all our tinplates were made in Great Britain until 1890, for which we annually paid to that country about twenty million dollars. This large sum would have been kept at home if we could have had legislation that would have been hostile to this British monopoly. It was destroyed for all time by the McKinley tariff of 1890.

# CHAPTER XVI.

### ABANDONED NEW ENGLAND FARMS.

THE free trade jeremiads a few years ago about the decline of agriculture in New England as a result of protection were very effectively answered by protectionists, who showed that there had been no decline in the prices received for New England agricultural products; that only stony and hilly farms had been abandoned; that there was nothing unnatural or unreasonable in wide-awake New England people abandoning these forbidding and unproductive farms and securing better farms in the Great West; and that, finally, there was a marked tendency all over this country to leave the farm and crowd into the towns and cities.

But this cry about abandoned New England farms, unfortunately for the argument which was associated with it, that protection had caused their abandonment, was not new. It was heard many years ago, when this country did not have a protective tariff or the semblance of one, namely, in the years when we were living under the Walker tariff of 1846 and the Guthrie tariff of 1857, both revenue measures, and revenue measures only, the latter remaining in force until it was succeeded by the Morrill tariff of 1861.

In the debate on the Tariff Commission bill in the House of Representatives in 1882 Mr. Carlisle, of Kentucky, said that there never has been a period of such general prosperity and growth in this or any other country as that which extended from 1850 to 1860, when the Walker and

Guthrie tariffs were in force. The distinguished Kentucky statesman surely could not have had in mind the condition of New England agriculture during the period of which he spoke. We are indebted to *Bradstreet's* for February 7, 1891, for the following bit of New England history, which illustrates the condition of New England's industries in Mr. Carlisle's golden age. The paper mentioned states that a gentleman of Franklin county, Massachusetts, discovered in 1890 a copy of an address delivered by his father to the farmers of Colerain in 1857 or 1858, in which he said:

"I have selected for my subject this evening 'The decline of the rural population of New England, of Franklin county, of Colerain in particular,' and I shall come to the conclusion, though reluctantly, that they have seen their best days. I need not waste your time by reciting voluminous statistics to prove this decline. Every intelligent man and woman sees it, and there is not a public speaker but refers to it, deprecates it, and offers his antidote. You have only to look before you to see it. . . . Look over this town and see the once expensive private dwellings going to ruin and into strange hands. They show that far back a high order of architecture existed here, and that a wealthy and prosperous set of farmers and mechanics occupied them. They are now in decay. The same thing can be seen, in a greater or less degree, in most of the rural districts of New England. Where is that long line of intelligent mechanics, with their half dozen apprentices and journeymen each, that were here? All are gone. The assessors' books show that the stock in Colerain has fallen off one-half in thirty years, and the farming inhabitants one-third, and it is still more glaring in some of the neighboring towns."

This address embodies precisely the sort of complaints which free traders have recently made. But there is this difference in the conditions prevailing in New England forty years ago and now: then low duties and Canadian reciprocity undoubtedly affected injuriously not only New England's agriculture but also all its varied industries; now New England is prosperous under protection beyond all previous experience.

# CHAPTER XVII.

## CHEAPENING THE NECESSARIES OF LIFE.

SELFISHNESS and the free trader becloud the question of cheap prices. The mechanic who is selfish wants a high price for his skill and labor but is not distressed if he can buy all the products of the farm at very low prices. Upon the other hand the farmer who is selfish wants high prices for his wheat and corn, his cattle and hogs, his potatoes and apples, but he insists that trace chains, blankets, clothing, farm implements, and everything else which he does not produce shall be sold to him at low prices, and the lower the prices the better he is pleased. The professional man who is a free trader and the non-producer who lives on a fixed salary or a fixed income of any kind want everything cheap —the products of the farm and the products of the shop. All of the demand for cheapness is of the character we have described. It would not be worthy of any notice but for the efforts of demagogues to magnify it into a political issue.

The free trade propagandist, who believes that cheapness is the chief good, can have no real sympathy with either the farmer or the mechanic, for he must know that the products of the labor of both must command good prices or they can not themselves be well rewarded for that labor. His appeals for cheapness, therefore, logically imply low wages and cheap men. He evades this conclusion, however, by so framing his appeals that they are never comprehensive of the whole community. He endeavors rather to set class against class. He tells the farmer that he pays too much for his trace chains, his blankets, his clothing, and his farm implements, and he tells the mechanic and the manufacturer that the wool which the farm produces should be cheaper than it is, even if it should come from abroad. This is what Mr. Cleveland did in his famous message of 1887. The teachings of that message and Mr. Cleveland's other public utterances on economic questions greatly contributed to the building up of the Populist party, which was at the outset but little else than the selfish movement of a class.

If the selfishness to which the free trader appeals were the governing motive of all men this would be a sorry world to live in. But it is not and can not be. Unfortunately for the mission of the free trader the people of this country who regard individual and class selfishness as a cardinal virtue are not in a majority or likely to be. If individual and class selfishness could dictate the economic policy of the United States next year or the next it would soon bring its own punishment. Individuals and classes would prey upon one another. Prosperity would vanish and chaos would come. Something approximating this condition occurred in the period from 1893 to 1897, when Mr. Cleveland's theories were more or less in force.

Yet there is a cheapness which may be had without degrading labor or setting class against class. It is the cheapness which results from a diversification of industries and the consequent employment of all the faculties of the human mind and all the aptitudes of the human hand. With every man profitably employed in doing that which he can do best it must follow that mechanical skill will be perfected and invention stimulated, so that cheapness will come from an increase of power in converting raw materials into finished products. This is precisely what happened in this country during the years which followed the passage of the Morrill tariff of March 2, 1861, and it is precisely what was denied to us during the time when we had a revenue tariff prior to 1861. The good results of this method of cheapening products continued with us even through the Cleveland depression. The inventive genius and the mechanical skill of our people have been so wonderfully developed since 1861 that we now rank with the most advanced of all the nations in the perfection of our mechanical processes and in the excellence of our products. And how greatly have we cheapened these products! If we have not yet succeeded in cheapening some manufactured products as much as they have been cheapened abroad it is because we have paid higher wages to our workingmen; we have not cheapened flesh and blood to the European level.

Mr. Cleveland and those who agree with him in demanding cheaper and still cheaper goods, and who really constitute themselves public enemies by their efforts to set class against class in this country, completely and deliberately ignore the cheapening effects of the protective policy against which they persistently declaim. They never tell the farmers who listen to them how much trace chains, and blankets, and clothing, and farm implements have been cheapened during the last thirty or forty years. They never tell any of their hearers how much steel rails and all iron and steel products, glassware, pottery, carpets, furniture, and textile fabrics have been cheapened in that period, nor how much more of any manufactured product a dollar will now buy than it would have bought when we were compelled to buy it from a foreign manufacturer. Everything that we now make in this country is very much cheaper than before our protective policy was firmly established in 1861. All the cheapness of manufactures that we enjoy is the result of protection; none of it can be credited to a tariff for revenue only.

But cheapness is not the chief good of our people, even when secured as the result of our protective policy. Employment is of first importance to the mechanic; a market for his crops is of first importance to the farmer. One reason why farming has been overdone in the West is because the depression in our manufacturing industries from 1873 to 1879 and in other years of hard times has led thousands to try farming who would have preferred to receive good wages as mechanics. What comfort is it to the farmer if he has good crops and the wages of mechanics everywhere are so low that they can not pay good prices for farm products? And what comfort is it to the unemployed mechanic that the necessaries of life are cheap if his wages have entirely ceased? He would prefer that they should be higher in price if his wages could only be restored. Both the farmer and the mechanic must in the end see that selfishness which thinks only of the welfare of individuals and classes will not pay.

# CHAPTER XVIII.

### CAPITAL THE FRIEND OF LABOR.

HENRY C. CAREY was fond of quoting the following extract from a report made by a British Parliamentary Commission in 1854, and which we have already quoted in a preceding chapter: "The laboring classes generally in the manufacturing districts of this country, and especially in the iron and coal districts, are very little aware of the extent to which they are often indebted for their being employed at all to the immense losses which their employers voluntarily incur in bad times *in order to destroy foreign competition and to gain and keep possession of foreign markets.* . . . The large capitals of this country are *the great instruments of warfare* against the competing capital of foreign countries." And Mr. Carey was never at a loss for vigorous words of condemnation of this piratical British policy, which has never been abandoned.

The policy of British manufacturers, frankly avowed in the above words, rendered necessary in this country a defensive policy for our struggling manufacturing industries, and in this fact alone we have ample justification of our protective policy. If British manufacturers were to undertake to systematically stamp out the industries of this country our people could do no less than resent and resist their selfish schemes.

But our present purpose is not to call attention to the necessity of a protective policy for this country as a measure of defense against foreign aggression, but to paraphrase the extract above given for the consideration of American workingmen. Let us imagine an American Congressional Commission making the following report: "The laboring classes generally in the manufacturing districts of the United States are very little aware of the extent to which they are often indebted for their being employed at all to the immense losses which their employers incur in bad times. The large capitals of this country are the great instruments in the defense of American labor against the competing capital of foreign countries in our markets and against all other unfriendly or unfavorable influences."

Is not all this literally true? How could many of our manufacturing industries have survived the panic of 1873 to 1879 if they had not rested upon a solid financial foundation which enabled them to sustain the shock of heavy losses which we all know they then experienced? How could many of these industries have lived through the depression of 1883 to 1885 and the panic of 1893 and the subsequent years of depression if they had not been fortified by the possession of large financial resources in the hands of resolute and courageous men? Where would poor men look for employment during a forbidding winter if it were not for the rich men who are often worried from day to day to obtain the money that is needed to pay wages to these same poor men? How helpless, indeed, are all poor men in our day who have no rich men to lean upon!

Instead of the workingmen of this country, or any part of them, joining with free trade orators and editors in the denunciation of capital as their enemy when it goes into the hands of a few rich men who are their own countrymen they should be thankful that these rich men are indeed their countrymen, who use their capital, no matter how obtained, in employing American labor, and that they are not foreign money kings, employing their capital in breaking down American industries. The more capital this country has the more labor will be employed, and the better the fight we can make for the upbuilding of American industries when, as has often happened, duties on foreign products are too low to be adequately protective, or when a financial panic or a prolonged period of business depression threatens the most serious consequences. Capital in large masses, unjust as it often is, is, after all, the mainstay of our industrial prosperity. If we had no more rich men in this country today than we had a quarter of a century ago we would be far behind in the race for industrial supremacy and the workingmen of this country would be poor indeed.

Nor should those who are now poor forget that most of our rich men were once themselves poor men, a fact which should encourage them to believe that they also may some day be capitalists. The way is open in this country to most industrious men to become capitalists in a small way by saving their earnings and prudently investing them. Opportunities to own a home are presented in this country which do not exist in any other country, and we know of no better way to become a capitalist than by buying a home and refusing to pay rent to a landlord. Then there are savings banks in which small savings may grow to large sums, and railroad and other securities in which money saved from going the way of the saloon-keeper and the race-course will yield sure dividends which also will help to make capitalists of thrifty workingmen.

But there are times and conditions, to which we have alluded, when it may be frankly admitted that money can not be laid away in any form—when employment is not always to be obtained and when wages are low. At such times the workingman must devote his energies to the task of simply supporting himself and his family until better times come. To do this and to keep out of debt may be a work of much difficulty, but it can be done in all cases except where there are special hardships to be borne.

There is, however, one supreme remedy for the hard times which this country occasionally experiences and which no legislation can wholly prevent. That remedy is economy in personal and household expenditures. The working people of this country must sooner or later learn to practice this virtue, and the sooner it enters into the daily life of every man and woman who is not in affluent circumstances the better. The American people can not form an exception to the general rule, the general law, which has come down to us from the ages, that those who would have must save and those who would save must practice self-denial. What profit is there to the laboring man who receives good wages if he spends part of them in the saloons or allows others to spend them foolishly? High wages are desirable, of course, but high wages and a lack of economy and good management will produce less desirable and satisfactory results than low wages that are carefully expended.

One of the saddest thoughts which come to the earnest advocates of the protective policy in this country is the reflection that the high wages which protection usually assures to our people are too frequently squandered at the beer saloon or wasted in bad housekeeping and in servile imitation of the habits of the rich. The sinful waste of American kitchens is of itself a deplorable spectacle. In any hundred homes that may be taken for illustration, outside of the slums of our large cities, it may be safely assumed that, between injudicious buying, bad cooking, and bad serving, enough food is habitually wasted to supply the tables of another hundred households. We are certainly the most wasteful people in the world in the matter of buying and cooking our daily food. We might learn from the French if we would the nourishment that is in a bowl of good soup prepared from inexpensive materials, and from the same people the staying qualities of a loaf of bread that is well made. We might also learn from the same provident people how to make a little bit of fuel go a long way. And common sense should teach the poor man who can not own a home of his own that he ought not to live in a house the rent of which is beyond his means.

All this is a story as old as the oldest of us. But the need of economy among all who work for daily wages appears to be especially necessary at this time of extravagant and wasteful habits of living. Instead of complaining of the exactions of capital American workingmen should seriously inquire whether they have themselves made the best use of their opportunities and of the wages that have been paid to them.

## CHAPTER XIX.

### OUR COLONIAL IRON INDUSTRY.

BEGINNING with an abortive attempt at ironmaking on Falling creek, Virginia, in 1622, and with a successful attempt at Lynn, Massachusetts, in 1645, the manufacture of iron was fully established before the Revolution in all the original thirteen colonies except Georgia. Historic names are associated with our colonial iron industry. Mordecai Lincoln, of Scituate, Massachusetts, from whom Abraham Lincoln was directly descended, was the principal owner as early as 1703, in company with his brother, Daniel Lincoln, of the Bound Brook Iron Works, not far from Hingham. Augustine Washington, the father of George Washington, was engaged in the manufacture of pig iron at Accokeek Furnace, in Stafford county, Virginia, at the time George Washington was born, in 1732, and he retained his connection with this furnace and with other iron enterprises of the Principio Company, of Maryland, until his death in 1743. His iron interests were continued in the Washington family down to the Revolution. Several signers of the Declaration were colonial iron manufacturers, as were also two of the most notable officers of the Continental army, General Nathanael Greene and Colonel Ethan Allen. In 1742 Benjamin Franklin invented the Franklin stove, which is still in use in some old Pennsylvania houses.

In his *Statistical View of the Commerce of the United States*, published in 1816, Timothy Pitkin says that near the beginning of the eighteenth century "the colonists began also to introduce sundry manufactures, for their own consumption, such as woolen and linen cloths, iron, hats, paper, etc. This excited the jealousy of the British manufacturer," and complaints were made to various departments of the parent government that the new enterprises were injurious to British interests and asking that they be suppressed. In 1731 Parliament so far listened to these complaints as to direct the Board of Trade and Plantations to make a report "with respect to laws made, manufactures set up, or trade carried on in the colonies, detrimental to the trade, navigation, or manufactures of Great Britain." The report was promptly made in the following year, the leading facts contained in it being derived from replies to interrogatories sent by the board to the governors of the different colonies. These replies admitted that unimportant manufactures had been "set up," including the manufacture of iron.

The Governor of Massachusetts Bay stated that "there had been for many years some iron works in that province, which had afforded the people iron for some of their necessary occasions, but that the iron imported from Great Britain was esteemed much the best and wholly used by the shipping, and that the iron works of the province were not able to supply the twentieth part of what was necessary for the use of the country." The report further mentioned that, "by late accounts from Massachusetts Bay," it appeared that there were in that province "several forges for making bar iron, and some furnaces for cast iron or hollow ware, and one slitting mill, and a manufacture for nails."

The report contains some information contributed by "the surveyor general of His Majesty's woods," who writes that "they have in New England six furnaces and nineteen forges for making iron," and that the people of New England "make all sorts of iron work for shipping." Bancroft says that these furnaces and forges had been "set up" as early as 1719 and that they were "a terror to England."

The Governor of Rhode Island wrote that "there are iron mines there, but not a fourth part iron enough to serve their own use," "but," says the report, "he takes no notice of any manufactures there."

The foregoing is all the view this report gives of the extent of the iron industry in the colonies in 1731. Notwithstanding these official statements we know from other and authentic sources of information that iron was made in New Jersey, Pennsylvania, Delaware, Maryland, Virginia, and North Carolina before 1731, but it does not appear to have been made in New York until after that year, or in South Carolina until 1773. Nor was the iron industry successfully established in Virginia until about 1715, fully a hundred years after this colony was founded.

Mr. Pitkin remarks of the period in colonial history covered by the Parliamentary inquiry of 1731 that "the making of pig and bar iron had become an object of some consequence in the colonies." The responses to this inquiry from which the above extracts have been taken and the statement by Bancroft constitute the earliest statistical record of the extent of the American iron industry.

The production of pig iron and bar iron in the colonies was encouraged by England soon after 1731 because she did not have a sufficient supply of these crude articles of her own manufacture, owing to the scarcity of charcoal, which was the only fuel then used in making iron. Pig iron and bar iron were exported from the colonies to England in the first half of the eighteenth century, and shipments of these articles to the mother country attained considerable proportions in subsequent years. But the mother country always discouraged the manufacture in the colonies of the more finished forms of iron and of all kinds of steel. England preferred to keep at home all manufacturing enterprises like those mentioned, that she might sell their products to the struggling colonists on the Atlantic coast at a good profit. In 1759 Israel Acrelius, the Swedish missionary to the Swedish settlements on the Delaware, said that "no one is allowed to make nails." But the colonists had made a start in the manufacture of the prohibited articles, as well as considerable progress in the manufacture of pig iron and bar iron, so that when the Revolution came they were prepared to make all the iron and steel munitions of war and other articles of iron and steel that were needed.

The causes of the virtual neglect of the iron industry in Virginia during the first hundred years of its existence as an English colony, from the early part of the seventeenth century to the early part of the eighteenth century, appear to have been the strong bent of its people toward agricultural pursuits and particularly the cultivation of tobacco, their consequent disinclination to build up towns and cities in which only the mechanic arts can flourish, and the practical absence of iron ore in the lower reaches of the Tidewater region, which was for many years the only part of the colony that was open to settlement. When the iron industry finally obtained a foothold in Virginia in the early part of the eighteenth century it was on the upper waters of the Rappahannock river, where iron ore was found in abundance.

Upon the other hand, Massachusetts, Rhode Island, and Connecticut successfully established the iron industry early in their colonial history because their people were more inclined to mechanical employments and to gather together in towns than those of Virginia; because the soil and climate of New England were not so well adapted to agricultural pursuits as the soil and climate of Virginia; and because iron ore was found near the sea-coast, where the first settlements were located. So, also, the first iron works in New Jersey were located near the sea-coast, in Monmouth county.

The ore which the pioneer iron manufacturers of New England and New Jersey first used was bog ore, which was found in abundance in the swamps and ponds near the sea-coast. It was exclusively used in New England during the whole of the seventeenth century and the early part of the eighteenth. In the latter century "rock ores" were found in the western part of New England which gave better results than the bog ores. In that century hard ore was also found at a few places in New England near the sea-coast. Before the close of the eighteenth century bog ore of superior quality was taken in considerable quantities to the eastern parts of Massachusetts from Egg Harbor, in New Jersey, for use in blast furnaces.

The bog ores of New England were chiefly used in the production of hollow-ware and other castings direct from blast furnaces, sometimes called foundries, but bar iron was also made from them. In New York, Pennsylvania, Maryland, and Virginia the pioneers in the manufacture of iron paid more attention to the production of pig iron for conversion into bar iron in refinery forges than the early New England manufacturers. Indeed they in part supplied New

England with bar iron and also with pig iron for its forges. The explanation is that these colonies had better ores than the bog ores of New England, and could make from them better bar iron, whether the ores were first smelted in furnaces or were directly converted into bar iron in bloomaries. Bar iron was, however, made in all the colonies in bloomaries as well as in refinery forges, although there never were many bloomaries in Pennsylvania and Maryland. The term bloomary was synonymous in the early days in this country with Catalan forge. Few forges and bloomaries are now left.

During the colonial era our iron industry was confined to the production of iron for domestic and simple mechanical purposes, except the pig and bar iron that were exported. There were no railroads, no locomotives, no freight and passenger cars, no iron or steel bridges, no iron or steel ships, no iron or steel buildings, no heavy pumping or hoisting machinery, no steam engines, no telegraph wires, and no wire fences. Pots and kettles, skillets, andirons and sad-irons, clock weights and stoves, and mill irons and plow points were cast at the furnaces. Nails were made by hand, generally from rods which were slit in slitting mills. Thomas Jefferson required about a dozen of the younger slaves owned by him to make nails, and it is recorded that "they made about a ton of nails a month at a considerable profit." But little steel was made, and most of the tools used were imported. All the fuel used in the iron industry was charcoal, and all the power used was water power. There were no rolling mills for bar iron; all the bar iron that was made was hammered under tilt-hammers and trip-hammers.

Considerable progress was made before the Revolution in the manufacture of axes, hoes, sickles, scythes, such machinery as was in use, and other finished products, and while the war continued a fresh impetus was given to their manufacture in all the colonies. Camp kettles for the Continental army were manufactured from sheet iron hammered at the forges. Cannon and cannon balls were cast at the furnaces. New England was most prominent in the manufacture of finished products throughout the whole of the eighteenth century, its people very early displaying a liking which they still retain for the reproductive branches of the iron industry. How much the country at large was dependent upon them for iron products of skilled workmanship is shown by an incident in the early settlement of Ohio. In 1789 the crank for the first saw-mill built in Ohio was carried by pack-horses over the mountains to the Youghiogheny river, and thence shipped by water to its destination on Wolf creek, sixteen miles from Marietta. It weighed 180 pounds, and was made in New Haven, Connecticut, for the New England Ohio Company.

The exhaustion of its bog ores and the increasing scarcity and dearness of charcoal closed many of the blast furnaces in the eastern parts of New England soon after the beginning of the present century, and at a later day other furnaces in the western parts of New England were closed because of the scarcity of charcoal and the high price of other fuel. New England is, therefore, no longer prominent in the manufacture of pig iron because its command of the raw materials is no longer absolute. Producing a scanty supply of pig iron, and having to depend largely on outside sources for its supply of mineral fuel, it was but natural that the rolling-mill industry of New England should also decline and that its steel industry should make but slow progress. All the bloomaries of Western Vermont have been abandoned because of the scarcity of charcoal and the wastefulness of the bloomary method of making iron.

New York and New Jersey have not maintained their colonial prestige as iron and steel manufacturers; relatively it may be said that they have retrograded. The scarcity of charcoal and the absence of mineral fuel within their borders have impeded their progress. Both States ship iron ore to their neighbors. Pennsylvania has been the first in the list of all our iron and steel manufacturing States since colonial days, attaining this distinction about 1750.

Maryland and Virginia were very active in the manufacture of iron in colonial times. Both of these colonies and North Carolina, as well as Pennsylvania and some other colonies, shipped iron to England before the Revolution. Long before that event hoes made in Virginia and North Carolina were sold in New York. With many furnaces and bloomaries North Carolina long continued to supply most of its own iron wants, both before and after the Revolution, and South Carolina had a flourishing iron industry on its northern border immediately after the Revolution.

There are now only two furnaces in North Carolina, one of which, a new furnace, has never been in blast. Of its numerous bloomaries only one is left. South Carolina presents a yet more remarkable instance of decadence in the manufacture of iron. Iron was made in this State for many years, commencing before the Revolution. As late as 1856 there were eight furnaces, three rolling mills, and two refinery forges in South Carolina. After the civil war the fires in all its iron works died out, and since then iron has not been made in any form within the limits of the State.

# CHAPTER XX.

## REMARKABLE DEVELOPMENT OF OUR IRON AND STEEL INDUSTRIES SINCE 1860.

AFTER the Revolution our iron and steel industries were slowly and spasmodically developed for many years, owing chiefly to the severity of foreign competition, which was only occasionally checked by friendly tariff legislation. For more than half the period from the inauguration of our present form of government in 1789 down to the beginning of our civil war in 1861 the duties on iron and steel were not sufficient to afford adequate protection to our iron and steel industries. With the enactment of the Morrill protective tariff on March 2, 1861, and with the added stimulus of the civil war, our iron and steel industries at once entered upon a period of extraordinary development, which, with some interruptions, has continued to the present time, greatly surpassing the development of like industries in any other country.

Our blast furnace practice has been completely revolutionized since 1860 by the introduction of more powerful blowing engines and improved hot-blast stoves, by the increased height and width of the furnaces, and by the general use of bituminous coke and of richer and purer iron ores, the latter coming chiefly from the Lake Superior region. About 1852 David Thomas, of Catasauqua, Pennsylvania, introduced powerful blowing engines at the furnaces of the Lehigh Crane Iron Company at Catasauqua, which increased the pressure of the blast to double that which was then customary in England. The results were so surprising that other furnacemen followed his example, but it was not generally copied until after 1860. The Player hot-blast stove was introduced into the United States in 1867 or 1868, the Whitwell hot-blast stove in 1875, and the Siemens-Cowper-Cochrane stove in 1877. In 1865 not more than 100,000 tons of coke were consumed in the production of pig iron in this country, but now nearly all our pig iron is produced with this fuel, the consumption of coke in our blast furnaces amounting in 1895 to more than 9,000,000 tons. In 1860 only 114,401 tons of iron ore were shipped from the Lake Superior mines, but in 1895 there were shipped 10,438,268 tons. As a result of all these changes we have recently made in one year more than ten times as much pig iron as we made in any year immediately prior to 1861, and with a smaller number of furnaces in active operation. In 1860 we made 821,223 tons of pig iron, and in 1890 we made 9,202,703 tons. In 1895 we made 9,446,308 tons. Our blast furnace practice is conceded to be the best in the world.

The total production of steel in the United States in the census year 1860 was reported to have been 11,838 tons, part of which was blister steel and the remainder crucible steel, both of which were products of very old manufacturing processes. We had just commenced the manufacture of crucible steel. In 1864 the manufacture of Bessemer steel in this country was successfully undertaken, and in 1868 we made our first open hearth steel. In 1895 our production of all kinds of steel, chiefly Bessemer and open hearth steel, was 6,114,834 tons. Like our blast furnace practice, our Bessemer steel practice is the best in the world, and our open hearth and crucible steel practice is not behind that of our rivals.

In the rolling and forging and founding of iron and steel, in the manufacture of heavy as well as light machinery of iron and steel, and in the adoption of labor-saving appliances in the mining and shipment of iron ore and for the handling as well as the production of iron and steel this country has always kept pace with the world's progress, and in many particulars it has shown the superiority of its methods over those of all other countries.

It was not until 1867 that we began to substitute Bessemer steel rails of domestic manufacture for iron rails, although small lots of Bessemer steel rails were imported in 1864, 1865, and 1866. In 1872 we made 808,866 tons of iron rails, which was the largest yearly product ever attained, and only 83,991 tons of Bessemer steel rails. We continued to make more iron rails than steel rails until 1877, but in that year iron rails fell behind steel rails, and ten years later, in 1887, we made 2,119,049 tons of steel rails, virtually all of which were Bessemer rails, and only 20,591 tons of iron rails. In 1895 we made 5,810 tons of iron rails. Our iron rail industry, which attained its maximum growth in 1872, is now practically extinct. So completely have steel rails taken the place of iron rails in this country that in 1895, according to *Poor's Manual,* 87.8 per cent. of the total railroad track of the United States had been laid with steel rails. This change has taken place chiefly within the last fifteen years. In 1880, according to the same authority, iron rails still formed 70.9 per cent. of our total railroad track.

As late as 1890 the making of heavy armor plates was an untried industry in this country, but to-day our heavy armor plates are the best in the world. Our first armor plates were made by the Bethlehem Iron Company in 1890, and soon afterwards armor plates were also made by the Carnegie Steel Company. The Russian Government has purchased American-made armor plates in preference to those made in European establishments. The rapid strides which this country has made in the building of steel merchant vessels for ocean and lake service and in the building and armament of a new navy reflect the highest credit upon our steel manufacturers as well as upon our shipbuilders. The great progress that has been made in late years in this country in the construction of steel bridges and in the substitution of iron and steel for wood in the erection of public and private buildings, particularly the very high buildings that are now to be seen in all our large cities, could not have taken place if our iron and steel manufacturers had not first demonstrated their ability to produce the structural forms required and at low prices. It is within the bounds of probability that the production of structural steel in this country, embracing beams, beam girders, zee bars, tees, channels, angles, and plate girders, will soon amount to a million tons annually. Excluding plate girders our production of structural steel in 1895 amounted to 517,920 tons.

In Alexander Hamilton's celebrated report in 1791, when he was Secretary of the Treasury, the claim was made that "the United States already in a great measure supply themselves with nails and spikes." The nails and spikes referred to were all made by hand labor, many of them in chimney corners. Nail-cutting machines had not yet been perfected. It was not until near the end of the first quarter of the present century that we made any considerable quantity of nails with the cut-nail machines with which the present generation is familiar. Until 1883 all our cut nails were made of iron, but in that year we began to make them of Bessemer steel, and in the same year steel wire nails began to come into use as a substitute for cut nails. In 1895 nearly all our cut nails were made of steel, but the quantity of cut nails produced had fallen far below that of wire nails, the production for that year being as follows: cut nails, 2,129,894 kegs of 100 pounds; wire nails, 5,841,403 kegs.

It may be doubted whether many persons realize the magnitude of the steel wire industry of this country. The 5,841,403 kegs of wire nails manufactured in 1895 were the equivalent of 260,777 tons. About as many tons of steel wire for fencing were also produced in 1895. The manufacture of wire rope is another leading branch of our steel wire industry, and so also has been the manufacture of telegraph and telephone wire, which is now made chiefly of copper. Electric railways also require large quantities of steel wire as well as copper wire. We did not make the steel for wire until after 1860. The wire cables for the Brooklyn bridge, which was completed in 1883, were made of American steel.

Closely related to our steel wire industry is our wire rod industry. It had an existence many years ago for the production of iron wire rods, but with the increased use of steel for various purposes for which wire rods are the raw material the demand for iron wire rods declined and the demand for steel wire rods increased. As late as 1875 we made very few steel wire rods. In 1883, when it was proposed to increase the production of steel wire rods by increasing the duty on foreign rods, the objection was made that we could not in a reasonable time supply our own wants for wire rods even if the duty were made more protective. The duty was increased in that year. In 1888 we made 279,769 tons of iron and steel wire rods, and in 1895 we made 791,130 tons, virtually all of which in both years were made of steel.

Our tinplate industry, the youngest of the industries belonging to the American iron trade, is wholly the creation of the last few years. Its marvelous growth is shown in the following summary from official statistics of our production of tinplates and terne plates during the five fiscal years beginning with July 1, 1891, and ending with June 30, 1896: Fiscal year 1892, 6,092 tons; fiscal year 1893, 44,562 tons; fiscal year 1894, 62,153 tons; fiscal year 1895, 86,519 tons; fiscal year 1896, 137,156 tons. This progress was made during a period which embraced several years of severe financial depression, accompanied by a sharp reduction in 1894 in the tinplate duty. While we have been so rapidly developing our tinplate industry we have developed with equal rapidity the manufacture of black plates, or sheets, to be tin-coated or terne-coated.

It is only just to say that the marvelous progress of our iron and steel industries since 1860 could not have been possible if we had not in the meantime opened one after another the rich iron ore mines of the Lake Superior region and gradually year after year substituted Connellsville coke for other fuel in the blast furnace. Other ores, notably the cheap ores of some of the Southern States, and other coke, notably that of Alabama and the Pocahontas Flat Top region, have in recent years contributed largely to our production of iron and steel, but it is nevertheless true that without Lake Superior ores and Connellsville coke we would still be in vassalage to Europe for many iron and steel products.

Natural gas has played an important part in the manufacture of finished forms of iron and steel since 1874, when it was first used in this country in puddling and heating furnaces and in the generation of steam. In 1886 every rolling mill and steel works in Allegheny county, Pennsylvania, 55 in all, used natural gas as fuel, and in the same year natural gas was used in 13 other mills and steel works—in nearly all exclusively. In 1887 there were 96 mills and steel works which used natural gas as fuel either wholly or in part, and in 1889 there were 104, but at the beginning of 1896, owing to the exhaustion of many sources of supply, there were only 89. The number must soon decline. The aggregate consumption of natural gas in the iron and steel works of the country is growing less and less from year to year. It is worthy of note, however, that the development of our iron and steel industries has been greatly promoted by the use of this ideal fuel, and that our tinplate industry especially owes much of its original and present activity to the use of natural gas in Indiana and some other States.

The rapid development of our iron and steel industries since 1860 could not, of course, have been possible without the aid of skilled metallurgists and engineers, who have in turn been largely indebted to our scientific and technical schools, yet it is remarkable that it was not until after the opening of the period under consideration that the chemical analysis of iron ores, blast furnace fuel, pig iron, and finished products received general attention. In 1860 James C. Booth, a noted Philadelphia chemist, was unable to induce the ironmasters of Eastern Pennsylvania to contribute jointly the sum of $1,200 to have the iron ores used by them analyzed by Mr. Booth. In the spring of 1863 William F. Durfee established a well equipped laboratory in connection with the experimental Bessemer steel works at Wyandotte,

Michigan, which is believed to have been the first chemical laboratory connected with any steel works in this country, if not in the world. As late as 1866, when J. Blodget Britton established his "ironmasters' laboratory" in Philadelphia, few furnacemen ever thought of having their raw materials or pig iron analyzed. Now practically all iron ores and pig iron in this country are sold by analysis, or upon reputation established by analysis, and chemical as well as physical tests are required in all sales of finished iron and steel which are subjected to extraordinary strain or pressure. It is also remarkable that pyrometers were not used in this country to measure the temperature of blast furnaces until 1862, when Edward Brown, of Philadelphia, introduced an English pyrometer, which was succeeded in 1869 by improved pyrometers of his own invention.

One result of the improvements that have taken place in the manufacture of iron and steel in this country since 1860 has been the partial or complete abandonment of time-honored methods of production which could not compete with the new methods. In 1860 only iron was used in the production of bars, rods, plates, sheets, and rails, and the puddling furnace was an indispensable agency in their manufacture. To-day the puddling furnace is second in importance to the Bessemer converter and to the open hearth furnace, both of which will encroach upon it more and more from year to year. The Danks puddler, from which so much was expected from 1870 to 1875, is never mentioned. The cementation furnace for making steel and the slitting mill for making nail rods survive only as curiosities. The blast furnaces that were run by water have nearly all gone. Except for special purposes the day of small furnaces is over. Forges for making bar iron from pig iron disappeared about 1860, but forges for making blooms, billets, and bars direct from the ore and blooms from scrap iron and pig iron have made a more vigorous struggle for existence, yet nearly all of these have also disappeared. As late as 1850 there were more pig iron and scrap iron forges in Pennsylvania than rolling mills, and as late as 1876 there were more iron ore forges in New York than rolling mills. In that year there were 27 forges in New York which made iron directly from the ore; there are now only 7, and not all of these are actively employed. For many years after 1860 there were more iron ore forges than rolling mills in several Southern States; there were hundreds of these forges, making small quantities of wrought iron directly from the ore, before 1860; but in 1896 there was only one active forge of this character left, Helton Forge, at Crumpler, in Ashe county, North Carolina. At the Exeter Steam Forge, in Berks county, Pennsylvania, bar iron is still hammered from charcoal blooms and wrought scrap iron, and this is the only forge that is left where bar iron is now hammered for the general market.

So numerous were forges in this country before they were supplanted by rolling mills and modern steel works that the Hon. Abram S. Hewitt made them the subject of a very neat compliment to American ironmasters in a speech at the dinner of the Iron and Steel Institute at New York, in October, 1890. Mr. Hewitt said that "for more than a hundred years, when there were few places of entertainment in this country, the traveler, when he set out on a journey, used to ask, 'How far is it to the next forge?' because there entertainment for man and beast was always to be found without money and without price."

The low prices at which steel rails of home manufacture have been sold to our railroad companies will serve as an illustration of the cheapening of all iron and steel products in this country since we began the manufacture of steel in large quantities under the stimulus of the Morrill tariff and its supplements. When it was proposed in Congress in 1870 to place a protective duty of $28 a ton on imported steel rails Mr. Kerr and Mr. Marshall, prominent members of the House of Representatives, earnestly protested against the proposed duty because it would so increase the cost of foreign steel rails that our railroad companies could not afford to import them. The average price of Bessemer steel rails in this country in 1870 was $106.75 a ton, in currency. The duty of $28 a ton was imposed in that year and the price of steel rails fell in five years to an average of $68.75 a ton, and it has never since risen above these figures but has steadily fallen in most of the succeeding years. In the whole of the year 1894 the price was $24 a ton, and in the early part of 1895 it was $22 a ton, or less than a cent a pound. In the latter part of 1895 and in 1896 it was $28 a ton, which is exactly the amount of the duty that was imposed in 1870, and in 1897 the price fell for a few days below $17 a ton.

During the whole of the important period under review the extension of our railroad system has been the leading commercial factor in building up our iron and steel industries. Our railroads have called for large quantities of iron and steel for rails, bridges, cars, locomotives, and other purposes. At the close of 1860 there were in this country 30,626 miles of steam railroad which were completed and in operation, and at the end of 1895 there were 181,021 miles, these being the figures of *Poor's Manual*. With the exception of 64.74 miles of elevated railroad in New York and Brooklyn the mileage of elevated and street railways is not included in the above figures for 1895. *The Street Railway Journal* for July, 1895, gives the aggregate track mileage of these railways in that year as 13,588 miles, including the New York and Brooklyn and other elevated roads.

But, while full force should be given to the tremendous demand which all our railroads have made upon our iron and steel works, our bridge works, our car and locomotive works, our car wheel works, and our machine shops and foundries, the fact is equally worthy of consideration that a large part of our railroad mileage could not have been built if our iron and steel manufacturers had not been encouraged by the protective policy to increase their facilities for the production of iron and steel, and if the competition between these manufacturers had not greatly reduced the prices of their products, most notably of steel rails, as has already been shown.

The statistics of pig iron production by Great Britain show how much more rapid has been the progress of our pig iron industry since 1860 than that of our rival. Great Britain produced almost as much pig iron in 1860 (3,826,-752 tons) as the United States produced in 1880, (3,835,-191 tons,) and yet, notwithstanding the fact that we started so far behind in the race, we made in 1890 more pig iron than Great Britain had made in any previous year or has since made. Her maximum production (8,659,681 tons) was attained in 1896; our production in 1890 was 9,202,703 tons; in 1892 it was 9,157,000 tons; and in 1895 it was 9,446,308 tons.

Our production of Bessemer steel rails exceeded that of

Great Britain in 1879, and we have ever since retained the leadership in this branch of the steel industry. Beginning with 1884 we have continuously led our great rival in the production of Bessemer steel ingots, and since 1890 we have been uniformly in advance of Great Britain in the aggregate production of all kinds of steel.

In our Annual Report for 1896 there was presented a table which gave the production of pig iron and steel in all countries in 1895. This table showed that this country's percentage of the world's production of these essentials of modern civilization was then as follows: pig iron, 32.71 per cent.; steel, 37.17 per cent. In the same year our percentage of the world's production of iron ore was 27.03, and of coal it was 29.77.

The magnitude of our iron and steel industries may also be seen in the statistics for the census year 1890. The whole number of establishments engaged in the production of pig iron, the production of crude steel, the rolling of iron and steel, and the production of iron blooms and billets in the United States in the census year 1890 was 719; the capital invested was $414,044,844; the number of employés was 175,506; the amount of wages paid was $95,736,192; the miscellaneous expenses amounted to $18,214,948; the cost of materials used was $327,272,845; and the value of all products was $478,687,519. The statistics given do not include the operation of our iron ore mines, which are an essential part of our iron and steel industries, and which in the calendar year 1889, which was also the census year for iron ore, employed $109,766,199 of capital and 38,227 workmen. Nor do they include the capital invested and the wages paid in the production of coal and coke for use at our iron and steel works, or the capital employed and the wages paid in the transportation of raw and finished materials.

The iron and steel industries of this country, as well as all other productive industries, were greatly depressed during 1893 and 1894, owing to causes which need not be here explained. There was no notable advance in iron and steel prices until after the close of the first quarter of 1895. Then followed the short-lived boom of 1895, during which demand increased and prices advanced. The year closed with slackened demand and reduced prices, which conditions were continued and intensified in 1896 and far into 1897.

The abnormally low prices which prevailed in 1893 and 1894 and again in 1896 and 1897 should not again be possible. During the former period the best furnace coke that this country can produce was sold on cars at 85 cents per ton of 2,000 pounds, and the best Lake Superior Bessemer ores were sold at less than $3 per gross ton delivered at Cleveland. If these raw materials had not been sold at the low prices mentioned the prices of pig iron, steel billets, steel rails, and other iron and steel products could not have fallen so low as they did. During the years 1896 and 1897 gray forge pig iron at Pittsburgh fell to $8.50 per ton and Bessemer pig iron in the same market to $9.25 per ton. Steel billets at Pittsburgh fell below $14 per ton in 1897.

Now, what may reasonably be predicted of the future of our wonderful iron and steel industries? It has been shown how rapid and substantial has been their development since 1860, how courageously we have invested our capital in establishing new branches of these industries, how promptly we have adopted new methods of manufacture, and how quickly we have responded to the demand for iron and steel for new uses. While we have made this creditable record as producers of iron and steel we have steadily improved the quality of all iron and steel products and as steadily reduced the prices at which they have been sold. It may be stated with confidence that our iron and steel manufacturers will meet the mechanical and commercial problems of the future as courageously and successfully as they have met those of the past.

It may safely be assumed that the protective policy of our fathers will be maintained in sufficient force to preserve the home market for the home producers of iron and steel, as well as for the producers of other products. The recent industrial depression, following the panic of 1893, has again shown the folly of any attempt to abandon the policy of protecting home industry against foreign competition. Granting, then, that our iron and steel manufacturers will continue to control the home market, will that market continue to consume our iron and steel products in quantities sufficient to maintain our iron and steel industries in healthy activity, barring, of course, periods of industrial depression which no foresight and no legislation can wholly guard against?

We think that there can be no doubt that the recently developed use of steel in the construction of public and private buildings will continue to grow from year to year. Among the advantages that are claimed for structural steel is its cheapness. Steel will also continue to be a favorite material in bridgebuilding. We will continue to turn out a large annual product of steel rails, but chiefly for renewals and extensions of railroad track already laid, and not chiefly for the construction of new railroads, nor of electric railways for passenger traffic, important as both these sources of demand must continue to be. We have built all the trunk lines of railroad that we now need, and our cities and large towns are supplied with electric railways. There will be an increased demand for iron and steel in the building of cars and locomotives and for the various appliances of electric roads. Whether we greatly increase our naval strength or not we will continue to require large quantities of structural steel in the construction of lake and ocean vessels. Our new tinplate industry will require continually increasing quantities of steel from year to year, our steady increase in population of itself contributing largely to this result. The use of cast iron pipe and of wrought iron and steel pipe must also increase with our increase in population. This increase in population will also enlarge the market for stoves, agricultural implements, cut and wire nails, wire fencing, and hundreds of other articles composed wholly or in part of iron or steel. Our aggregate consumption of iron and steel must certainly increase as the years roll on.

# CHAPTER XXI.

### REVELATIONS OF AN OLD LEDGER.

In a little while the writers and orators of this country will be busily engaged in recounting the achievements of the nineteenth century, of which only a few years remain. We will be told of the great progress that the world has made during this wonderful century in the advancement of the arts and sciences, in the spread of civil and religious liberty, in the diffusion of general intelligence, in the multiplication of social comforts, and in many other ways. We will, for instance, have our attention called to the fact that the world has produced and consumed more iron and steel in the last half of the nineteenth century than in all previous time, and also to the fact that the methods of manufacturing iron and steel in that half century were chiefly the inventions of that period, and were so revolutionary of old-time methods that they would amaze and dumbfound the ironmasters of even two generations ago if they could come back and witness them in operation.

Without anticipating the comparisons and the eulogies of the writers and orators referred to we propose to note some of the old ways of doing business in an iron town in Pennsylvania at the beginning of the century that is so near its end. They furnish a contrast with present business methods that is just as great as that afforded by the old and the new methods of manufacturing iron and steel. For the facts we shall present we are indebted to an old ledger which has recently come into our possession and which escaped the destruction of the Johnstown flood in 1889. The ledger contains accounts of sales made and of credits entered by Isaac Proctor, a merchant of Johnstown in the early years of the present century, and a record of other business transactions by Mr. Proctor. His store was located on Main street, immediately opposite the site of the present Presbyterian church.

Isaac Proctor was a native of Bedford county, Pennsylvania. He settled at Johnstown, "at the forks of the Conemaugh," when it was a mere hamlet of log houses, about the year 1800, in which year the town was laid out by Joseph Johns, a Swiss Mennonite, into streets and alleys, building lots, public squares, and other reservations. But the name that was then officially given to the new town was Conemaugh and not Johnstown, the latter name being substituted for the former in 1834. We have before us a letter dated at Conemaugh on April 27, 1832. Settlements had been made at Johnstown before 1800 by German and Swiss farmers. For a number of years after 1800 the town was almost exclusively inhabited by people of German and Swiss origin.

Isaac Proctor was not only a country merchant but he was also the owner of a warehouse on the north bank of Stony creek, below Franklin street, in Johnstown, which was maintained for the express purpose of receiving and storing bar iron from the forges of the Juniata Valley, which bar iron was hauled to Johnstown over the Frankstown road and thence shipped in large flatboats to Pittsburgh by way of the Conemaugh, Kiskiminetas, and Allegheny rivers. There were other warehouses near that of Isaac Proctor which were maintained for precisely the same purpose. The flatboats were built at Johnstown or at points farther up the

Stony creek and as far south as the mouth of Ben's creek, three miles away. A large business was done far into the present century in the shipment of Juniata iron by flatboats from Johnstown. At first and for many years these shipments embraced only bar iron, but subsequently and down to the opening of the Pennsylvania Canal to Johnstown in 1830 they embraced also blooms and pig iron, all made with charcoal. As the navigation of the streams mentioned was as yet wholly unimproved shipments could only be made during high water, and even then experienced pilots were required to prevent the boats from going to pieces on the rocks and riffles in which the Conemaugh river particularly abounded. Occasionally a boat was wrecked. In one disaster at Richards' Falls two lives were lost. Much of the hauling over the Frankstown road was done in the winter, and February and March, when the spring "break-up" took place, were favorite months for sending the flatboats to Pittsburgh, which was one hundred miles away. The boats were sold at Pittsburgh and the crews walked home.

Keelboats were also used on the Conemaugh and Kiskiminetas rivers, but they were used chiefly in the salt trade, the Conemaugh salt works beginning about forty miles west of Johnstown. The first salt works on the Conemaugh date from about 1814. In A. J. Hite's *Hand Book of Johnstown*, printed in 1856, it is stated that the first keelboat built at Johnstown was built by Isaac Proctor in 1816. Keelboats, which passed from the Conemaugh and Kiskiminetas into the Allegheny, brought back return cargoes from Pittsburgh.

The merchandise accounts in Mr. Proctor's ledger are chiefly for the years 1808 and 1809, occasional entries coming down as late as 1810, 1811, and 1812. The warehouse accounts are for the years 1816, 1817, and 1818. As is usual in ledger accounts the prices of merchandise are not often given. It is, however, very remarkable that all the merchandise accounts are kept in pounds, shillings, and pence. The pound character (£) is used. Dollars and cents are nowhere mentioned, although our federal coinage was authorized in 1792 and silver dollars were coined as early as 1794. The dollar mark ($) does not appear in any of the merchandise accounts. That business should have been transacted in British or colonial currency in an interior town in Pennsylvania as late as 1812 is a discovery for which we were not prepared. We can not understand why the British system of computing values was continued in that interior town so long, nor is any light thrown upon the value of a pound in dollars and cents at Johnstown in 1812, or upon the forms of currency that were used when payments were made in "cash." John Holliday closed his account with Mr. Proctor in June, 1811, when he is credited with a payment of £32 16s. 4d. in "cash;" in January, 1811, Patrick Dempsey closed his account by giving his note for £6 10s. 3d.; in 1812 William Fulford closed his account by giving his note for £2 6s. 1d.; and in the same year John Grosenickle closed his account by giving his note for £1 1s. 2d. In 1808 John Grosenickle is credited with £1 11s. 9d. for hauling a load of maple sugar to Bedford. There are other entries in the same denominations.

Another revelation of this old ledger is just as remarkable as the use of pounds, shillings, and pence until 1812. The warehouse accounts of bar iron received and shipped in 1816, 1817, and 1818 are kept in tons, hundredweights, quarters, and pounds, the ton representing 2,240 pounds, the hundredweight 112 pounds, and the quarter 28 pounds. The teamsters who hauled bar iron over the Frankstown road are credited in tons, hundredweights, quarters, and pounds, and shipments to Pittsburgh are entered in the same terms. In ordinary commercial transactions neither iron nor any other commodity has been weighed by hundredweights and quarters forming fractions of a gross ton at any time within our recollection, the usage being to weigh only by tons and pounds, and it is really very surprising that the early English custom should have prevailed at Johnstown at so late a day as we have mentioned. Charges for storage in 1816, 1817, and 1818 appear, however, to have been paid in dollars and cents, as we find several charges in 1818 in these denominations. We have also found within the leaves of the ledger a bill against Isaac Proctor which reads as follows: "Juniata Forge, 16th December, 1818. Mr. Isaac Proctor Bot of Peter Shoenberger 2 qrs. 1 lb. Bar Iron, @ $0.08c—$4.56." Juniata Forge was located at Petersburg, in Huntingdon county, and was built about 1804. In 1814 or 1815 it passed into the hands of Dr. Peter Shoenberger.

The numerous entries in Mr. Proctor's ledger make clear the fact that large quantities of bar iron were shipped at Johnstown by flatboat in 1816, 1817, and 1818. He did a large warehousing business, and other owners of warehouses were probably active competitors. The aggregate tonnage shipped by Mr. Proctor, which was chiefly on account of Dr. Shoenberger, amounted to several hundred tons annually. Some of Mr. Proctor's single shipments amounted to 16 and 19 tons. Some of these shipments were made "in my own boat," which was probably a keelboat. Pittsburgh antiquarians may be interested in learning that the consignees of bar iron at Pittsburgh were Richard Bowen & Co., Robert Alexander, Allen & Grant, Charles McGee, J. Whiting, Robinson, McNickel & Wilds, Irwin & George, and Thomas Jackson.

From other sources than the old ledger we add some other facts which show the prominence of Johnstown as an iron centre early in the present century.

John Holliday built a forge at Johnstown, on the north bank of the Stony creek, about 1809, for the manufacture of bar iron from Juniata blooms and pig iron, but we find no mention in Mr. Proctor's ledger of any shipments from this forge. The dam of this forge was washed away about 1811, and subsequently the forge was removed to the north bank of the Conemaugh, in the Millville addition to Johnstown, where it was operated down to about 1822, Rahm & Bean, of Pittsburgh, being the lessees at this time. In 1817 Thomas Burrell, the proprietor at that time, offered wood-cutters "fifty cents per cord for chopping two thousand cords of wood at Cambria Forge, Johnstown." The forge would appear to have been in operation from 1809 to 1822.

In 1807 or 1808 Shade Furnace was built on Shade creek, in Somerset county, about fifteen miles southeast of Johnstown, and in 1820 Shade Forge was built near the furnace. As early as 1820 bar iron was shipped to Pittsburgh from Shade Forge. Much of the iron from this forge was hauled to Johnstown for shipment down the Conemaugh, but some of it was shipped in flatboats directly from the forge. Pig iron was also hauled to Johnstown from Shade Furnace for shipment to Pittsburgh. But there was another early forge, which was still nearer to Johnstown, on the Stony creek, about half a mile below the mouth of Shade creek, known as Mary Ann Forge, which shipped bar iron to Pittsburgh at a still earlier day, and perhaps as early as 1811. Richard Geary, the father of Governor John W. Geary, was the manager of the forge for about one year, and was supercargo of a load of bar iron which was shipped from the forge down the Stony creek, the Conemaugh, and other streams to Pittsburgh. Garret Ream lived at the mouth of Ben's creek and built boats which were loaded at Johnstown, but he also shipped iron direct from Ben's creek, and it is probable that some of this iron came from Mary Ann Forge, Shade Furnace, and Shade Forge.

About 200 pounds of nails, valued at $30, were made at Johnstown by one establishment in the census year 1810. About this time an enterprise was established at Johnstown by Robert Pierson, by whom nails were cut from strips of so-called "nail iron" with a machine worked by a treadle, but without heads, which were added by hand in a vise. The "nail iron" was obtained at the small rolling mills in Huntingdon county and hauled in wagons to Johnstown.

The chief interest of this old ledger consists in its revelation of the fact that large quantities of Juniata bar iron were shipped to Pittsburgh from Johnstown as early as 1816. Earlier shipments were made by water from Johnstown to the same destination, probably as early as 1800, but the ledger of Isaac Proctor shows conclusively that these shipments had attained large proportions in 1816, 1817, and 1818, in which years bar iron had not yet been made at Pittsburgh. Next in importance among the facts disclosed by Mr. Proctor's ledger is the survival at Johnstown down to 1812 of the British system of computing values, and the survival down to 1818 of the now long disused hundredweights and quarters.

# CHAPTER XXII.

## THE EARLY HISTORY OF PITTSBURGH.

THE prominence which Pittsburgh has attained as the centre of the iron, steel, bituminous coal, and glass industries of the United States, and as the centre of the world's iron and steel industries, justifies some reference in these pages to its early history and to the prominent part which Washington bore in shaping that history. The dates which we shall give have been verified from trustworthy sources.

The selection of the forks of the Ohio river, formed by the junction of the Monongahela and the Allegheny rivers, as a suitable place for the erection of a fort, was made in 1753 by George Washington for the mutual benefit of the Ohio Company and the colony of Virginia, which latter Washington officially and directly represented. The Ohio Company was composed chiefly of Virginians, and of this company Lawrence and Augustine Washington, half brothers of George Washington, were members. The company was organized to engage in trade with the Indians west of the Alleghenies and to secure valuable grants of land. It received the encouragement and support of the Virginia authorities because the territory it expected to occupy was claimed as a part of Virginia. In November of the year above mentioned Washington visited the forks of the Ohio while serving as a commissioner from Governor Dinwiddie, of Virginia, to the French commandant in Northwestern Pennsylvania. He says in his journal that he thinks the point at the junction of the two rivers "extremely well situated for a fort." The Ohio Company had previously selected a site for a fort on the left bank of the Ohio river, two miles below the junction of the Allegheny and the Monongahela rivers, at a place now known as McKee's Rocks, but Washington condemned this selection for reasons which are mentioned in his journal. His judgment was superior to that of the company, which approved his choice, as did also the Virginia authorities. In February, 1754, by direction of the Governor of Virginia, a company of Virginia militia, commanded by Captain William Trent, undertook the erection of a fort in the forks, in aid of the plans of the Ohio Company and to establish the jurisdiction of Virginia, but from this work the militia were driven in April by a large body of French and Indians, who immediately began and completed the erection of a fort at the same place, which they called Fort Duquesne, in honor of the Governor-General of Canada.

In the month of April, 1754, Washington was sent by Governor Dinwiddie with a small force of Virginians, which was subsequently increased, to the support of the Virginia company under Captain Trent, but before reaching Western Pennsylvania he learned that the half-completed fort at the forks of the Ohio had fallen into the hands of the French. Washington pushed on toward the mouth of Redstone creek on the Monongahela river, where he could establish a base of operations against the French and await reinforcements. A strong force of French and Indians was promptly dispatched from Fort Duquesne against Washington's small command, intercepting him before he reached his destination. The battle of Great Meadows, in Fayette county, Pennsylvania, about seventy-five miles southeast of Fort Pitt, was fought by the contending forces on July 3, 1754, which was followed by Washington's capitulation, his first and only surrender, and by the abandonment of his expedition. These events mark the beginning of the final contest between the French and the English for the control of the country west of the Alleghenies. (In 1767 Washington bought a tract of 234 acres which included Great Meadows, and he owned this tract at his death in 1799.)

An ineffectual attempt was made in 1755 by a force of British regulars and provincial troops to drive the French from Fort Duquesne, which resulted in the defeat of General Braddock near the site of the present Edgar Thomson Steel Works. Three years afterwards, in November, 1758, Fort Duquesne fell into the hands of the British and their provincial allies under General Forbes, the French blowing up the fort and disappearing, some of them pushing off in their boats down the Ohio and up the Allegheny, while others marched overland to Erie, then known as Presqu' Isle.

Washington was present at Braddock's defeat, as is well known, but he was also present when Fort Duquesne fell into the hands of General Forbes in 1758, which is not so well known. In December, 1758, a new fort was built at the forks and named Fort Pitt, in honor of William Pitt, the British Secretary of State. In 1759 and 1760 the construction of a more formidable fortification, to take the place of the first Fort Pitt, was commenced and practically completed by General Stanwix, the new fort being also named Fort Pitt. This fort was entirely completed by Colonel Bouquet in 1761, who added in 1764 a block-house, or redoubt, which is still standing.

In 1763 the conspiracy of the Western Indians under the

leadership of Pontiac was formed and a fierce border war ensued, during which Fort Pitt was for many weeks besieged by a large body of Indians and successfully defended by the garrison under command of Captain Ecuyer, a native of Switzerland. While the siege was in progress Colonel Bouquet, also a native of Switzerland, commanding the British and provincial forces in Pennsylvania, Maryland, and Virginia, and whose headquarters were then in Philadelphia, moved from Carlisle to the relief of Fort Pitt with about five hundred men in his command. In August the Indians temporarily abandoned the siege of Fort Pitt and attacked Colonel Bouquet's command at Bushy Run, in Westmoreland county, about twenty-five miles east of Pittsburgh, but after an engagement of two days were defeated, with severe loss on both sides. This defeat resulted in raising the siege of Fort Pitt. Sufficient importance has never been attached to the battle of Bushy Run. It was one of the most sanguinary and eventful engagements between whites and Indians that was ever fought.

In 1772 Fort Pitt was abandoned by the British and its garrison was withdrawn by General Gage, the commander of the British forces in America. The fort was subsequently occupied by Continental troops during the Revolution. For some years after the Revolution Fort Pitt was occupied by United States troops as a protection against the Indians, but by 1791 the fort had been entirely abandoned and a large part of it was torn down in the fall of that year. Late in the same year orders were issued to Major Isaac Craig to build a new fortification at Pittsburgh, and this structure, situated on the left bank of the Allegheny river, about a quarter of a mile above Fort Pitt, and which was called Fort Fayette, was finished and occupied by a garrison in 1792. This fort was used in that year in the initial operations in General Anthony Wayne's expedition against the Indians, and it continued to be occupied by a garrison for several years afterwards, forming one of the frontier forts that were maintained to overawe the Indians. Thomas Ashe, an English traveler, says that a garrison was maintained at Fort Fayette when he visited Pittsburgh in October, 1806. The Allegheny Arsenal, at Pittsburgh, was completed in 1814, and Fort Fayette was doubtless abandoned about that time.

Returning to Fort Pitt, it is stated in Craig's *History of Pittsburgh*, in a description of the fort as it existed about 1796 to 1800, that "the ramparts of Fort Pitt were still standing, and a portion of the officers' quarters, a substantial brick building, was used as a malt house." From 1803 to 1806 the Methodists of Pittsburgh were accustomed to hold religious services "in a room of Old Fort Pitt," which is supposed to have formed a part of "the officers' quarters" mentioned by Craig.

The city of Pittsburgh occupies in part the site of Fort Duquesne, the French fortification, of Fort Pitt, its British successor, and of Fort Fayette. As early as 1758 settlers began to gather about Fort Pitt, and in 1760 there were 149 men, women, and children outside the fort. In 1764 lots and streets in the immediate vicinity of the fort, occupying four squares, were laid out. The frontier settlement at Fort Pitt was known by the name of Pittsburgh as early as 1758, as appears from a letter from General Forbes and from Christian Frederick Post's journal. In 1769 the Manor of Pittsburgh was surveyed and reserved by the Penns, the proprietaries of the province. In 1770 Washington visited

Pittsburgh while on his way to the Kanawha Valley, in the present State of West Virginia. In his journal Washington says: "We lodged in what is called the town, distant about three hundred yards from the fort, at one Semple's, who keeps a very good house of public entertainment. The houses, which are built of logs, and ranged in streets, are on the Monongahela, and I suppose may be about twenty in number and inhabited by Indian traders." In the siege of Fort Pitt, in 1763, the houses which had then been built outside the fort were all burned. In 1783, after the treaty of peace, the proprietaries decided to sell the lands within the Manor of Pittsburgh, the first sale being made in January, 1784. In that year the town of Pittsburgh was surveyed into streets, alleys, and lots, and sales of lots were rapidly made. Writing in his journal under date of December 24, 1784, Arthur Lee says: "Pittsburgh is inhabited almost entirely by Scots and Irish, who live in paltry log houses." In 1786 Pittsburgh is said to have contained thirty-six log houses, one stone house, one frame house, and five small stores. The town had grown but little since Washington's visit in 1770. Even after 1786 it had a very slow growth.

Down to 1779 Virginia claimed and attempted to exercise jurisdiction over that portion of Southwestern Pennsylvania which is now embraced in Allegheny, Washington, Fayette, and adjoining counties, but in that year commissioners from Virginia and Pennsylvania agreed to the boundaries between the two States which have since been observed, and in 1780 the agreement was formally ratified by the Legislature of each State. Under the Virginia claim the settlement at Fort Pitt was embraced within the boundaries of Augusta county, Virginia, Staunton being then as now its county-seat. Under the Pennsylvania claim and down to 1788 Pittsburgh was included within the limits of Westmoreland county, its county-seat being Hannastown, but in that year Allegheny county was organized and Pittsburgh became the county-seat.

On April 22, 1794, an act of the Pennsylvania Legislature was passed incorporating the town of Pittsburgh into a borough. In 1796 Pittsburgh had a population of 1,395, and in 1800 the population was only 1,565. In 1810 it had increased to 4,768. On March 18, 1816, the borough of Pittsburgh was erected into a city. In 1830 the population was 12,568, in 1840 it was 21,115, and in 1850 it was 46,601. In 1845 occurred the great fire at Pittsburgh, which destroyed over one thousand dwellings, warehouses, stores, and other buildings, the loss amounting to about six million dollars.

In 1787 the town of Allegheny, opposite Pittsburgh, was "laid out by the order of the sovereign authority of Pennsylvania," with the intention of making it the county-seat of Allegheny county, but this intention was soon abandoned. Allegheny became a borough in 1828 and it was incorporated into a city in 1840.

The proprietaries of the province of Pennsylvania were fully aware as early as 1769 of the existence of coal at Pittsburgh. In a letter dated at London, January 31, 1769, Thomas Penn writes to his nephew, Lieutenant-Governor John Penn, as follows: "We desire you will order 5,000 acres of land to be laid out about Pittsburgh, including the town, which may now be laid out, and I think from its situation will become considerable in time; and that the land may be laid out to Colonel Francis and his associates, and other gentlemen of whom I wrote, as contiguous as it may be, and in regular right-angled tracts, if possible." On May 12 of the same year he writes to Mr. Tilghman respecting this survey, and says: "I would not engross all the coal hills, but rather leave the greater part to others who may work them." The difficulties between the mother country and her colonies prevented all these instructions from being obeyed. The Manor of Pittsburgh was, however, surveyed in 1769, as already stated.

In 1784, the year in which Pittsburgh was surveyed into building lots, the privilege of mining coal in the "great seam" opposite the town was sold by the Penns at the rate of £30 for each mining lot, extending back to the centre of the hill. This event may be regarded as forming the beginning of the coal trade of Pittsburgh. Soon afterwards the supply of the towns on the Ohio and Mississippi rivers with Pittsburgh coal became an established business.

Down to 1845 all the coal shipped westward from Pittsburgh was floated down the Ohio in flat-bottomed boats with the spring and fall freshets, each boat holding about 15,000 bushels of coal. The boats were usually lashed in pairs, and were sold and broken up when their destination was reached. In 1845 steam tow-boats were introduced, which towed coal barges down the river and brought them back empty. About 1845 Pittsburgh coal began to be used in Philadelphia, transportation being by way of the Pennsylvania Canal.

In 1786 *The Pittsburgh Gazette*, the first newspaper published west of the Allegheny mountains, was established at Pittsburgh. The first glass works at Pittsburgh were established in 1797, in which year Craig & O'Hara began the manufacture of window glass on a small scale. The first steamboat to run on the western rivers was built at Pittsburgh in 1811 and named the *New Orleans*, but prior to this year many other vessels had been built at Pittsburgh.

In 1792 George Anshutz built a small iron blast furnace on Two-mile run, within the present limits of Pittsburgh, but it was in operation only two years. Late in 1805 the first iron foundry at Pittsburgh was completed by Joseph McClurg and it was in operation in February, 1806. John and Mathew Stewart had a cut-nail manufactory in operation in September, 1805, which appears to have been the first in Pittsburgh. "Dorsey's iron" was for sale at Pittsburgh in October, 1805, by Thomas Cromwell. In April, 1807, E. Denny advertised "barr iron for sale, from Huntingdon and Centre counties, at a reduced price." In 1811 and 1812 the first iron rolling mill at Pittsburgh was erected by Christopher Cowan, but it did not make bar iron. In 1850 there were 16 iron rolling mills in Pittsburgh and its vicinity, with a capital of about $3,000,000, employing about 2,000 hands, and consuming about 65,000 tons of pig iron, blooms, and scrap. But there was not a blast furnace in Pittsburgh or its vicinity at that time, its first furnace not being built until 1859, if we except George Anshutz's little furnace on Two-mile run. Nor was the manufacture of steel at Pittsburgh in 1850 anything else than an infant industry.

In 1897 there were 30 blast furnaces in Allegheny county, all active, and 64 rolling mills and steel works. In 1896 Allegheny county produced more pig iron and rolled more iron and steel than the remainder of Pennsylvania, and it also rolled more iron and steel than the total product of Ohio, Illinois, and Indiana. In the same year it made over 23 per cent. of the country's total production of pig iron, over 41 per cent. of our total production of Bessemer steel, over 43 per cent. of our total production of open hearth steel, over 55 per cent. of our total production of crucible steel, and over 30 per cent. of our total production of rolled iron and steel. Abraham Lincoln well named it "the State of Allegheny."

The Nestor of the Allegheny county iron trade is the Hon. B. F. Jones, of Pittsburgh, the head of the enterprising firm of Jones & Laughlins, who has been actively and successfully engaged in the manufacture of iron and steel for more than fifty years. Much of the prominence that Pittsburgh has attained as an iron and steel centre is due to the creative and executive genius of Andrew Carnegie, who has built up at Pittsburgh the most extensive iron and steel enterprise in the United States and perhaps in the world. Mr. Carnegie has been ably assisted in the development of his vast iron and steel interests by his partner, Mr. Henry C. Frick, who had previously achieved a world-wide reputation by systematizing and greatly expanding the Connellsville coke industry.

So marvelous has been the development of the iron and steel and other industries of Pittsburgh and its vicinity, so excellent are its transportation facilities, and so great are the advantages afforded it by the possession of natural gas and cheap coal and coke, that the future progress of this industrial centre is certain to attract as much attention as its past achievements. Pittsburgh is an industrial wonder.

The information contained in this chapter concerning Fort Pitt and Fort Fayette has been mainly derived from Neville B. Craig's *History of Pittsburgh*, from Dallas Albert's *Frontier Forts of Western Pennsylvania*, and from T. J. Chapman's history of *The French in the Allegheny Valley*.

## CHAPTER XXIII.

#### THE RESTRICTION OF IMMIGRATION.

IMMIGRATION into the United States from 1789 to 1842 never exceeded 100,000 persons annually, and seldom came anywhere near that number, the nearest approach to 100,000 being in 1840, when the arrivals of alien passengers numbered 84,066; in 1841 they numbered 80,289. Down to and including 1855 immigrants do not appear to have been classified separately from other alien passengers, but virtually all such passengers were immigrants. The total number of alien passengers who arrived from 1789 to 1820 was about 250,000; from 1821 to 1830 the arrivals numbered 143,439; and from 1831 to 1840 they numbered 599,125. In 1842 they numbered 104,565. In the next two years the arrivals declined below 100,000 annually, but in the six succeeding fiscal years, ending on September 30, 1850, they rapidly increased, owing to the Irish famine, the revolutionary movements in various European countries, the demand in this country for labor to build railroads, and the discovery of gold in California. In the six fiscal years referred to the arrivals of aliens were as follows: 1845, 114,371; 1846, 154,416; 1847, 234,968; 1848, 226,527; 1849, 297,024; 1850, 310,004: total in six years, 1,337,310.

The six years from 1845 to 1850 mark the beginning of the flood of immigration which has ever since annually brought to our shores large numbers of persons of all classes and conditions from every clime under the sun. In the ten calendar years from 1851 to 1860 there arrived in the United States 2,579,520 immigrants and alien passengers; in the ten years from 1861 to 1870 the arrivals of immigrants alone numbered 2,450,520; in the ten years from 1871 to 1880 they numbered 2,944,695; in the ten years from 1881 to 1890 they numbered 5,176,212; and in the six years from 1891 to 1896 they numbered 2,513,051. In 1880 the arrivals for the first time exceeded half a million, numbering 593,703. In the next two years the wave of immigration rose still higher, the arrivals in 1881 being 720,045 and in 1882 reaching 730,349. In the three years mentioned the arrivals numbered 2,044,097—an astonishing total. During the one hundred and eight years from 1789 to 1896 the total number of alien passengers and immigrants who arrived in the United States was 18,369,813.

The census of 1890 showed that, of a total population of 62,622,250 in the census year 1890, exclusive of Indians, 9,249,547 were of foreign birth, as compared with 6,679,943 of foreign birth in a similar total population of 50,155,783 in the census year 1880. The percentage of our foreign born population in 1890 was 14.77, as compared with 13.32 in 1880.

As late as the Centennial year, 1876, very few immigrants came from Italy or from any of the Slavic countries, but in the two decades which have since elapsed the arrivals from Italy, Bohemia, Hungary, Russia, and Poland have aggregated about two millions. Of the immigrants arriving in 1876 Austria sent us 6,047; Hungary, 475; Italy, 2,980; Russia, 6,787 (principally Mennonites of German origin); and Poland, 854. Beginning with 1880 the arrivals from Italy and the Slavic countries rapidly increased. In the

## THE RESTRICTION OF IMMIGRATION. 179

six years from 1891 to 1896, inclusive, we received 1,040,614 immigrants from Bohemia, Hungary, and other Austrian provinces and from Russia, Poland, and Italy; 174,034 came from Bohemia and Hungary, 160,112 from other Austrian provinces, 282,387 from Russia, 67,700 from Poland, and 356,381 from Italy: total, 1,040,614.

From January 1, 1853, to June 30, 1888, a period of almost thirty-six years, 288,775 Chinese immigrants arrived in this country, of whom 279,885 were males and 8,890 were females. The largest number arriving in any year was in the fiscal year 1882, when 39,463 males and 116 females came. The effect of the passage of the several Chinese immigration acts, the first of which went into effect in August, 1882, has been very marked, the number of immigrants immediately declining, until in the fiscal year 1887 only 8 males and 2 females arrived in this country at ports of entry. In the fiscal year 1888 the arrivals at these ports amounted to 26, of which 21 were males and 5 were females. To the official figures since 1882 must be added an unknown number of Chinese immigrants who have illegally crossed the border from British Columbia and Mexico.

Opposition to the immigration of foreigners manifested itself over fifty years ago in occasional riotous demonstrations, chiefly directed, however, against Roman Catholics of Irish birth. In 1844 there was an outbreak in Philadelphia of intense hostility to the immigration of these persons and to all adherents of the Roman Catholic faith, which ended in a bloody riot. The waves of this outbreak extended to many other cities and to many towns and rural communities, and for a time there was a great deal of what was known as Native American sentiment throughout the country. It almost died out, however, during the Mexican war, and in the Presidential campaign of 1848, when a Mexican war hero was the successful candidate, we heard nothing of it. Strictly speaking this Native American sentiment partook more of the nature of religious persecution than of hostility to foreigners as such, although it embodied also a strong feeling of hostility to the granting of citizenship to foreigners of any faith until they had lived twenty-one years in the country. The immigration of paupers and criminals was also condemned by the Native American sentiment of 1844.

In 1852, when General Scott and General Pierce were the opposing candidates for the Presidency, there was a revival of interest in the Native American issues of 1844, but not enough to seriously influence the public mind. But in 1854 there was a fierce and widespread display of hostility to citizens of foreign birth and to all Roman Catholics, the principal ground of opposition being the assumed unfitness of either class to hold any political office. Such mottoes as "America for Americans" and "Put none but Americans on guard" were the shibboleths of the new party, which was popularly known as the Know Nothing party. In the year last mentioned it swept all opposition before it, and in 1855 it was still a powerful organization, but in 1856 it virtually gave way to the rising Republican party, which absorbed most of its members. The slavery question and soon afterwards the civil war left no room for religious prejudices or distinctions of birth. When the first shot was fired at Fort Sumter, on April 12, 1861, a new political issue, which swallowed up all others, was at once created. Opposition to immigration practically ceased also for the special reason that many foreigners fought in the Union ranks.

Many years have passed since Sumter was fired upon. In the main the country has been very prosperous during this period. But there have been intervals of serious business depression, and the causes of this depression have been much discussed and remedies for real or supposed evils have been anxiously sought. The conviction has gradually obtained a place in the minds of many of our people that all business depression in this country is greatly aggravated by foreign immigration, resulting in an over-supply of labor in all employments, especially in periods of depression. Unrestricted immigration is also responsible for the presence among us of thousands of idle and vicious foreigners who have not come here to work for a living but to stir up strife and to commit crime. It is also responsible for the attempt to naturalize upon American soil those two most pernicious foes of social order and national and individual well-being, namely, an unrestrained liquor traffic and a Sunday devoted to dissipation and amusements. It has also brought in its train a vast amount of the densest ignorance and of squalid poverty and incurable wretchedness, our great cities suffering the most from these enemies of a true civilization.

As one consequence of the unhealthy influences to which we have referred there has been within the last twenty years a revival of interest in one of the Native American issues of 1844 and 1854, namely, hostility to unrestricted immigration. It has not taken the form of opposition to foreigners because they are foreigners, as in other years, but of opposition to the immigration of contract laborers, paupers, criminals, socialists, illiterates, and all foreigners whose antecedents and practices tend to the subversion of the wholesome traditions and customs of our country. Many of our foreign-born citizens heartily sympathize with this sentiment. In 1882 we very wisely prohibited Chinese immigration. In 1885 we prohibited the importation of all contract laborers, although the act relating to this subject is robbed of much of its force by the ease with which contracts are made with immigrants after their arrival at New York. In 1891 we prohibited the immigration of paupers, criminals, and those who are mentally or physically diseased. These restrictive measures show the drift of public opinion a few years ago.

But more recently there has been manifested a widespread demand that these measures be supplemented by more vigorous restrictive legislation which will fully embody the principle that the people of this country should be more thoroughly protected against the unloading upon our shores of European paupers, criminals, mischief-makers, and European scum generally. This sentiment is not an echo of the proscriptive spirit of 1844 and 1854, but it will not be denied that, if the restrictions which the Native American party desired to place upon the immigration of paupers and criminals had been adopted and enforced when they were suggested and subsequently, our cities and large towns and our mining and manufacturing districts would not to-day be afflicted with persons that Europe is glad to get rid of.

The agitation for more restrictive immigration legislation resulted in the passage by the Fifty-fourth Congress of a bill imposing an educational test, which excluded, with limited exceptions, all persons who can not read and write the English language or some other language. This bill was vetoed by President Cleveland on March 2, 1897. In the House the bill was passed over the veto the next day by 193 yeas to 37 nays, but the consideration of the veto was not reached in the Senate before the final adjournment of Congress. The bill therefore failed to become a law.

It was well to preserve free territory for free men; it was well to emancipate our African slaves; but an equally important duty was neglected when we failed after the civil war to check the immigration into our country of persons who were in no way fitted to become American citizens.

Instead of checking undesirable immigration the Government of the United States encouraged unrestricted immigration until a few years ago. Land grants to railroad companies led to extraordinary efforts by steamship companies, in collusion with the land-grant companies, to fill the holds of their vessels with steerage passengers of every description. In 1871 the Treasury Department published a volume of about 250 pages, entitled *Information for Immigrants*, which was scattered broadcast over Europe, and which described in glowing terms the opportunities offered by this country to the people of other countries. It was a most mischievous publication. Some of the States have also scattered alluring advertisements throughout Europe, printed in several languages. The efforts of the railroad companies and of the steamship companies to stimulate immigration have not by any means been abandoned. Immigration should have been subjected to governmental regulation and restriction many years ago, when it first began to manifest evil tendencies, and it should never have been forced or stimulated by government land grants or in any of the other ways we have briefly described. As a nation we have had in the last thirty years an abnormal and unhealthy instead of a normal and healthy growth. One result is that we have no longer a homogeneous population as we had down to about 1840.

# CHAPTER XXIV.

### THE DRIFT OF POPULATION TO THE GREAT CITIES.

An evil of our day in the United States and in some other countries is the steady drift of population from the country to the city. The census of 1890 showed that nearly one-third of the people of this country then lived in cities having a population of 8,000 or over, and the drift from the country to the city has since doubtless increased. During the hundred years from 1790 to 1890 the proportion of our population residing in cities having 8,000 inhabitants or over increased from 3.35 per cent. to 29.20 per cent. The number of cities having a population of more than 8,000 increased from six in 1790 to 286 in 1880 and to 448 in 1890. There ought, however, to come a time when there will be a reaction from this tendency to desert the country and crowd into the cities. Much of the flitting from the country to the city which is continually taking place is the result of an obtuseness of vision which fails to discern where the advantages of the country end and the disadvantages of the city begin. With a clearer vision most of those who exchange the country for the city would remain where first their lot in life was cast—in the country town if not literally in the country itself. The hard lines of city life for millions of city poor, including those who are regularly employed but who find it hard to make both ends meet, must surely some day bring this clearer vision to other millions whose homes are "far from the madding crowd's ignoble strife."

Men do not now need to go to the city to secure for themselves and their families the advantages of polite society, good schools, libraries, lectures, and all home comforts and luxuries. These are now as accessible to the dwellers in most country towns and to most good farmers as to the dwellers in cities. Enterprising villages and towns now dot every State in the Union, and emulate with more or less success the social, business, and intellectual life of our great cities. The showy Queen Anne house, the daily newspaper, the telegraph, the telephone, and the latest fashions for dress are everywhere. That great civilizer, the railroad, leads the way to universal progress. The town upon a leading railroad route learns from the city, and the wide-awake farmer and his wife and children meet city influences whenever they go to town.

The fact is not so generally recognized as it should be that, by means of the wider circulation of money, consequent upon the extension of railroads, the opening of new mines, and the building of new factories and workshops, the comforts of life are more generally diffused in the country than in the cities. It is a fact well established that nowhere are there to-day such sunken eyes, such threadbare garments, such "looped and windowed raggedness," such utter destitution and wretchedness, such dire despair, as in the city. In country towns and in farmers' homes the city extremes of abject poverty and princely affluence are seldom found. There is greater pecuniary and social equality. Carpets now cover the floors of the humblest rural homes, and those who occupy these homes no longer dress in homespun, nor are many of them compelled to deny themselves the best food the farm and garden afford. All the little appliances, too, which tend to make home cheerful and to lighten the labors of those who have the keeping of the home are as accessible in the country as in the city and at prices within the reach of all. In most of the houses in small towns it is now possible to have all the heating and lighting and sanitary conveniences that are to be found in city houses.

Farmers particularly are large gainers by the progressive ideas of the last fifty years. Much of the severe labor that was once necessary to make the farm profitable is now rendered unnecessary by the numerous mechanical appliances that are everywhere in use. Not only labor but time also is thus saved, affording opportunity to old and young for study, for recreation, and for the cultivation of the graces and amenities of life. The improvements in agricultural implements have greatly contributed to the farmer's productive power, while the railroads and the manufacturing enterprise of his countrymen have given him, as a rule, a good home market for all that he has to sell—for every dozen of eggs, pound of butter, gallon of milk, and bunch of vegetables, as well as for the more important crops of the farm. With all these beneficent results of our advancing civilization he has no rent to pay and the tax-gatherer deals gently with his possessions. If he sometimes receives low prices for the products he has to sell he pays low prices for all that he has to buy. Hence he is usually prosperous, notwithstanding all that is said to the contrary, and with his prosperity come many of the advantages which make city life attractive. From few of these is he now debarred. Why should he seek comfort and happiness and the amplest development in the great city? He may have them where he is, for himself and his children, if he but make good use of his opportunities and be thoroughly in harmony with the spirit of the age in which he lives. Let the wide-awake farmer look around him!

Frequent intercourse between farmers and between farmers and those who live in towns is more easily accomplished now than formerly. There are better means of communication than once existed, although good roads are still sorely needed. The increasing number of farmers, notwithstanding the drift to the city, is gradually shortening the distance from one farmer's fireside to that of another, and our increase in population is multiplying towns and villages and bringing nearer to the farmer all the intellectual and social advantages which he and his family may derive from them.

Lectures have been mentioned as among the advantages of city life that are possessed by the country. Nearly every village in the land may have its course of literary or scientific lectures once a year if it will. The farmers' club, which is popular in many States and which should everywhere be established where farms are not too widely separated, is an enlargement of the lecture system that furnishes not only lectures and essays but also profitable discussions, social reunions, and exhibitions of the products of the farm and garden. The isolation and the loneliness of the farmer's life and its lack of inspiration to intellectual effort are old objections to living on a farm which the farmers' club is well calculated to remove.

Every town and village which has had an existence for fifty or a hundred years, and therefore has a history of its own, should establish and maintain a museum of natural curiosities and historical relics, and every town and village possessing a sufficient population, and whether old or new, should have a public library and at least the beginning of an art gallery. The museum could be joined to the library and the art gallery. If people in rural communities and small towns would only sit down to study this matter they would be surprised to discover how far a little money and effort will go in securing the objects mentioned, and with these objects attained they would soon be further surprised to witness their elevating and every way beneficial effects. There might, for instance, be fewer saloons if there were more town libraries and museums and art galleries.

When the rich men whose homes are in the city place their money and their influence, as many of them are now doing, in the scale in behalf of clean and wide streets, large and small parks, the planting of shade trees, and every other measure calculated to foster rural taste and to scatter rural delights among all classes of their fellow-citizens, and, above all, when they resolve to spend their summers in the quiet suburbs of a great city, they unconsciously pay a deserved tribute to the advantages possessed by the country and the country town and to the blessings which come to him who has made good use of these advantages.

In these days of widespread discontent with social conditions, which is perhaps more strongly marked among farmers and in small communities than in the cities, we entreat all who have homes of their own, either in the country or in the town of a few hundred or a few thousand inhabitants, not to lightly value the blessings which they owe to those homes. Be they ever so humble let their owners hold fast to them as if they were veritable palaces compared with the restricted accommodations and mean surroundings that characterize the large majority of the homes of a great city.

## CHAPTER XXV.

### THE WESTERN FARMERS' DISCONTENT.

THE Populist advocate sees but one side of the farmers' question, and that is the side of those who are discontented. He does not tell us of the far larger number of Western farmers who are contented with their lot and satisfied with their rewards. Nor does he impartially seek to discover how far the existing discontent is the result of causes which are beyond the farmers' control or anybody's control. That many farmers have not been prosperous may be frankly admitted, but the Populist makes a grave mistake when he assumes that this lack of prosperity is the result of bad treatment of the farmers by other classes of their countrymen. If he had not looked so exclusively at one side of his subject he would not have reached this unwise and unjust conclusion.

Most Populists make prominent the charge that the farmers have been injured by legislation in favor of other industries than that of agriculture, mentioning particularly our manufacturing industries, shipbuilding, and banking, while agriculture itself has received no special legislative privileges whatever. Admitting for the sake of argument that the allegation is true that special legislative privileges have been accorded to the manufacturer, the shipbuilder, and the banker, it does not follow that the benefits of these privileges have not been shared by the farmer.

If protective tariff legislation has built up domestic manufactures have not the mills and furnaces and factories and workshops created by this legislation greatly increased the demand for agricultural products? Have not the farmers' markets grown with the wonderful development of our manufacturing industries? Every intelligent farmer knows that protective tariff legislation has had just this effect. And he also knows that this legislation, by developing our resources and creating competition in all manufacturing pursuits, has cheapened the cost of transporting agricultural products to both domestic and foreign markets, cheapened the cost of agricultural implements, and cheapened the cost of everything that the farmer has to buy. We could fill these pages with figures to prove the cheapening effects of protective tariff legislation upon all manufactured products. If the results of this legislation to the farmer have been such as we have described what is there in that legislation that he has to complain of?

And so of such little legislation as we have had in the interest of American shipbuilding. By encouraging the building of American steamships and promoting the establishment of American steamship lines to foreign countries we have increased the facilities for transporting our surplus agricultural products to foreign markets. The farmer is really the chief beneficiary of this policy, for the more markets he has the better off he is. Our Government should help to establish steamship lines that would run to all parts of the world. This is what Great Britain has long done.

And so also of the special privileges which have been granted by Congress to national banks. Originating in the necessities of the Government when the very life of the nation was at stake these privileges have been continued in the interest of the whole people of the United States, to whom safe banking facilities and bank notes that are worth their face value are absolute necessities. The free banking law which has long been in force permits any community of commercial importance to have a national bank if it has sufficient enterprise and capital, and the original national banking law and its supplements guarantee the holder of every national bank note against any loss by the failure of the bank which issues it. How much better is this system for everybody, the farmer included, than the old wild-cat and red-dog system of banking, which gave us notes issued by irresponsible speculators in human credulity—notes that everybody dreaded to keep over night for fear that the banks which issued them would break before morning. Surely our national banking system has been of immense benefit to the farmer in enabling him to get good money for all the products of his farm.

Have special privileges, or, rather, has special legislation, been withheld from the farmer? The facts do not sustain this plea. We invite attention to a few subjects of national legislation which refute the argument that the farmer has been neglected by those who have made the country's laws.

The homestead law was enacted many years ago for the special benefit of farmers and of intending farmers who were not able to buy improved farms. By means of this law large sections in the West have been opened to agriculture and civilization, and thousands and tens of thousands of poor men have been enabled to secure for themselves and their families farms and homes which otherwise they never would have owned. That these farms might be tilled in peace the Government has protected their owners against Indian incursions by maintaining a standing army on the Indian frontier.

That the farmer with little money and his family might reach the Great West the Government adopted the policy of giving away millions of acres of beautiful prairie to corporations which would agree to build railroads through the empires that had been given to them. By means of these railroads the farmer with little money could first reach the farm that was waiting for him and which was to cost him nothing, or which he would buy from the railroad builders at a low price, and afterwards could send to a distant market the crops that would be grown upon his farm.

Many years ago the Department of Agriculture was established as a separate branch of the Government for the special benefit of the farmer. Seeds were given to him, books were printed for him, and the condition of his crops and his live stock and his chances of getting good prices for all that he had to sell were paternally and thoroughly inquired into. All this is done to-day—more of it to-day than ever. Even the control of the weather bureau has been transferred to this department largely for the benefit of the farmers. The head of this department has a seat in the President's Cabinet. The whole people pay the expenses of this separate department of the Government, amounting to millions of dollars annually. But there are no similar departments to care for the interests of manufacturers, miners, shipbuilders, or any other industrial classes of the country.

And, then, there are the agricultural colleges, for the education of farmers' sons and daughters, which are to be found in every State, and which were established and endowed by grants of public lands by act of Congress many years ago, the lands being the property of the whole people of the United States.

The interstate commerce law was enacted a few years ago with the special object of so regulating the freight charges on farmers' products that these charges should not become extortionate. Nobody else but farmers strongly urged the passage of this law, and they got just what they asked for.

Our protective tariff legislation has not been exclusively for the benefit of manufacturers. It has also been for the special benefit of farmers. The more important products of the farm have always in this legislation been protected against foreign competition. Our wool-growing industry has been almost wholly created by this legislation, while wheat, corn, oats, barley, butter, cheese, horses, cattle, and many other farm products have long been subject to protective duties which shield the farmer from Canadian and other competition. In the framing of the McKinley and the Dingley tariffs no duties received more careful attention than those which affect the farmers' products. The reciprocity features of these two protective tariffs were inserted chiefly to secure enlarged markets for all that our farmers have to sell. For the first time in the history of the country a bounty was authorized by the McKinley tariff to be paid directly from the public treasury to stimulate an agricultural industry, the production of sugar. The whole people of the country have had to pay this sugar bounty.

It is neither correct nor gracious, therefore, for Populists to assert, or to imply, that the interests of American farmers have been neglected in our protective tariff legislation, or that other classes of the community have been favored in this legislation at the expense of American farmers. Whatever may be the burdens of any of our farmers to-day they are not traceable to protective tariff legislation. Until the

Wilson tariff succeeded the McKinley tariff in 1894 American farmers received their full share of friendly legislation.

The cause of hard times for the farmers of the West lies deeper; there have been too many farmers for the markets that were at their command. By our land-grant policy the business of opening up new farms in the mighty West has been overdone, and excessive competition in wheat-growing and corn-growing has in recent years brought down the prices of both these products lower than they should have been. No right-thinking man wants any farmer to grow wheat for fifty cents a bushel or corn for twenty cents.

In what has been said above we have purposely avoided any reference to the alleged demonetization of silver as one of the causes of the discontent of Western farmers. That issue has been sufficiently discussed. The silver question, however, would never have been the bone of contention that it has been if Western farmers could have realized in recent years better prices for their products than they have received. That they did not realize better prices is due mainly to the fact that there has been an overproduction of agricultural products, just as there has been an overproduction of iron and steel and other manufactured products. The silver issue has simply served to emphasize the Western farmers' discontent. Our real trouble in late years has been overproduction of agricultural as well as manufactured products. Our capacity to produce has more than kept pace with our ability to consume.

## CHAPTER XXVI.

### HISTORY OF RECIPROCITY LEGISLATION.

As THE subject of reciprocity in our trade relations with foreign countries is virtually a new feature in our tariff legislation we give below the history of the insertion of the reciprocity policy in the McKinley tariff of 1890.

When the Ways and Means Committee of the House of Representatives framed the tariff bill which afterwards, with amendments, became the tariff act of 1890 it placed all sugar in the free list, except the very small quantity of refined sugar above number 16 Dutch standard that might be imported. At the same time, that our sugar industry should not lack protection, the committee provided a bounty of two cents a pound for the producers of cane, beet, and sorghum sugar testing at least 85 degrees by the polariscope. The bill made no reference to reciprocity. It passed the House on May 21, 1890, with the sugar bounty provision included. It was referred to the Senate Committee on Finance on May 23 and reported from that committee to the Senate on June 18, with amendments, but with the sugar bounty provision unchanged, except that it was made to apply to maple sugar. No reference was made to reciprocity. That feature was also omitted from a second revision of the bill by the Committee on Finance, which revision was reported back to the Senate on September 6.

On September 10 the bill passed the Senate, and it then for the first time contained the reciprocity provision, which was inserted at the instance of Mr. Blaine, the Secretary of State, supported by President Harrison. In the bill as it passed the Senate the House bounty of two cents a pound on sugar was left unchanged except that the maple sugar amendment was approved. In the conference committee the Senate reciprocity amendment was approved, but the sugar bounty was changed so that the producers of sugar testing 90 degrees and upwards should receive two cents a pound, while the producers of sugar testing less than 90 degrees and not less than 80 degrees should receive one and three-fourths cents a pound. In this form the bill passed both houses and became a law.

The sugar bounty provision of the tariff act of 1890 was an entirely new feature in our tariff legislation. We know of but one precedent for the payment of a bounty by the General Government for the promotion of any productive American industry. In the country's early history and until about the middle of the present century bounties were paid to promote our fishery industry, but they also promoted the building up of an American merchant marine and the training of sailors for the American navy, which were doubtless the principal objects the bounties were expected to accomplish. The *American Cyclopædia* says: "During the war with England in 1812–15 the British cruisers kept the fishermen from the distant fishing grounds. Many of them entered the navy, and the frigate *Constitution* was chiefly manned by them, while great numbers engaged in privateering."

There is no mention of reciprocity in any of the platforms of the Republican party prior to the Presidential campaign of 1892, when the Minneapolis Convention of that year indorsed "the Republican policy of reciprocity" which had been incorporated in the tariff act of 1890, but it did not mention the free sugar and sugar bounty policy which had been incorporated in the same tariff and which was the cause of the insertion in that tariff of the reciprocity policy, nor has a sugar bounty or any other bounty for the benefit of any of our productive industries ever been approved by a Republican National Convention. The reciprocity and sugar bounty legislation embodied in the tariff act of 1890 was, therefore, not only legislation which had not previously been recommended by a Republican National Convention, but the sugar bounty feature of that legislation has not since been approved by the same authority. It was not approved in the Minneapolis platform of 1892 nor in the St. Louis platform of 1896, and it finds no place in the Dingley tariff of 1897. The St. Louis platform approved of reciprocity. Here is an anomaly. Reciprocity and a sugar bounty, the latter a consequence of free sugar, were inseparable features of the tariff legislation of 1890, and yet one has been approved and the other has not been approved.

This country had experimented with the policy of reciprocity in two instances before the passage of the tariff act of 1890—a reciprocity treaty with Canada having been concluded in 1854 and continuing in force until 1866, and a reciprocity treaty with Hawaii having been concluded in 1875 and being still in force. Our experience with Canadian reciprocity was not satisfactory to this country, and the reciprocity treaty with Canada was abrogated at the instance of our Government. The reciprocity treaty with Hawaii was entered into for other than commercial considerations.

The reciprocity features of the tariff of 1890 not only applied to sugar but also to molasses, coffee, tea, and hides, but their principal application, and their only important application, was to sugar. A number of reciprocity treaties were negotiated by President Harrison with sugar-producing countries, as well as with other countries. These treaties were abrogated by the Wilson tariff of 1894, a Democratic measure. While they were in force the country lost in a period of great financial depression about $200,000,000 in revenue. The following table shows the receipts of the Treasury from duties on sugar in the three fiscal years immediately preceding the enactment of the tariff act of 1890 and in the three full fiscal years succeeding its enactment.

| Fiscal years. | Duties paid. | Fiscal years. | Duties paid. |
|---|---|---|---|
| 1888 | $50,647,014.17 | 1892 | $76,795.14 |
| 1889 | 54,896,437.38 | 1893 | 163,956.25 |
| 1890 | 53,985,873.85 | 1894 | 250,763.53 |

It is fair to assume that the total loss of revenue to the Treasury from sugar during the almost four years in which the tariff act of 1890 was in force exceeded $200,000,000 and averaged above $50,000,000 annually, in which figures we include the payments on account of sugar bounties in the fiscal years 1892, 1893, and 1894 and the fraction of the fiscal year 1895 extending from July 1 to August 28, 1894. These payments were as follows: 1892, $7,342,077.79; 1893, $9,375,130.88; 1894, $12,100,208.89; 1895, $966,185.84: total, $29,783,603.40.

Wise as was the tariff act of 1890 in nearly every particular we have always contended that it was most unwise in abandoning the sugar duties embodied in previous tariff legislation, and which had been a source of large revenue to the Treasury, and providing for the payment of a sugar

## HISTORY OF RECIPROCITY LEGISLATION. 199

bounty in lieu of the protection they had afforded to our sugar industry. Having passed the House these provisions concerning free sugar and a sugar bounty paved the way for the reciprocity amendment in the Senate; indeed they were the direct cause of it. Reciprocity treaties would not have been thought of in 1890 by Mr. Blaine and others if sugar had not been made free in the House bill.

The course of our export trade in iron and steel and manufactures of iron and steel in recent years, to which we will be excused for making special reference, does not indicate that this branch of our export trade was at all benefited under the late reciprocity treaties. The subjoined table gives the value of our exports of iron and steel and of manufactures of iron and steel in the calendar years from 1887 to 1896, inclusive, not including agricultural implements.

| Years. | Exports. | Years. | Exports. |
|---|---|---|---|
| 1887 | $16,235,922 | 1892 | $27,900,862 |
| 1888 | 19,578,489 | 1893 | 30,159,363 |
| 1889 | 23,712,814 | 1894 | 29,943,729 |
| 1890 | 27,000,134 | 1895 | 35,071,563 |
| 1891 | 30,736,507 | 1896 | 48,670,218 |

From this table it will be seen that our exports of the articles mentioned increased over 66 per cent. in the four years from 1887 to 1890 without reciprocity; that in the four years from 1891 to 1894 there was an actual decrease under reciprocity; and that in 1895 and 1896 there was a large increase over 1894 without reciprocity.

The Dingley tariff act of 1897 provides for two classes of reciprocity treaties which may be negotiated by the President. In the first class (section 3) may be included brandies, champagne and other wines, paintings and statuary, "argols, or crude tartar, or wine lees, crude," upon which the duties imposed by the Dingley tariff may be reduced to certain specified rates; also coffee, tea, and "tonquin, tonqua, or tonka beans, and vanilla beans," now in the free list of the Dingley tariff, upon which certain specified duties may be imposed if the countries producing these articles shall impose "unequal and unreasonable" duties on the products of the United States. The President alone is empowered to enter into reciprocal treaties with the countries producing these articles. No limit of time is placed upon the negotiation or continuance of treaties in this class. In the second class (section 4) may be included every article of foreign origin, other than those articles above mentioned, which is subject to duty in the Dingley tariff, upon which the duty may be reduced not more than 20 per cent., except that there may be transferred wholly from the dutiable list to the free list such goods, wares, and merchandise as are the "natural products of foreign countries and not of the United States." All such treaties are to be "duly ratified by the Senate and approved by Congress," and are to be entered into within two years from the passage of the Dingley tariff and to be for fixed periods not exceeding five years.

If any reciprocity treaties should be negotiated by the present Administration under the Dingley tariff they would hardly apply to sugar, which is again in the dutiable list, and from which source we are certain to continue to need a large revenue. Under the McKinley tariff the consent of the Senate to reciprocity treaties was not required, and under section 3 of the Dingley tariff it is not now required, but it will be noticed that the consent of the Senate and the approval of the House of Representatives (Congress) must first be obtained before any reciprocity treaties under section 4 of the Dingley tariff can go into effect.

The fatal error that is embodied in the reciprocity policy is its abandonment of the policy adopted by the fathers of the Republic of imposing duties at the custom-house that should be uniform in their application to the products of all countries. In lieu of this policy, which was established in our first tariff act, and which had been sanctified by one hundred years of successful trial, there was substituted in 1890 the British policy of variable commercial treaties, otherwise called reciprocity, and this was done not to protect and preserve the home market for home producers, which is the very essence of the protective policy of the fathers, but that foreign markets of less value than the trade of one of our great States might possibly be captured. How we lost our own markets and otherwise lost money by our reciprocity treaty with Canada while it was in force from 1854 to 1866 is told in the following extract from a speech in the Senate by Senator Morrill, of Vermont, on July 30, 1890.

"Our exports to Canada in 1855 were $20,828,676, but under the operation of reciprocity then commenced they dwindled in twelve years down to $15,243,834, while the exports of Canada to the United States increased from $12,182,314 to $46,199,470. When the treaty began the balance of trade had been $8,000,000 annually in our favor, and that paid in specie, but at the end the balance against us to be paid in specie in a single year was $30,000,000. Here was a yearly positive loss of over five millions of our export trade and a loss of thirty-eight millions of specie, all going to enrich the Canadas at our expense."

# CHAPTER XXVII.

### HOW SCHUYLER COLFAX ROSE TO BE VICE PRESIDENT.

THE House of Representatives of the Congress of the United States has had two Speakers who were newspaper editors by profession, Schuyler Colfax, of Indiana, from 1863 to 1869, and James G. Blaine, of Maine, from 1869 to 1875. For twelve years the popular branch of Congress was presided over continuously by these two editors. Concerning the first of these an interesting story has been told.

On Saturday evening, December 19, 1863, a company of gentlemen, composed exclusively of journalists and newspaper men, and representing all the political parties of the day, met Mr. Colfax at dinner at Willard's Hotel, in Washington. Mr. Colfax was present by invitation of his professional brethren, who desired in this formal way to do honor to him as a distinguished member of the American "fourth estate." The immediate occasion of the compliment was the elevation of Mr. Colfax two weeks previously to the Speakership of the House of Representatives, the first instance in the history of the Government of an editor having been selected to fill that responsible position. After the cloth was removed the president of the evening, Samuel Wilkeson, then the Washington correspondent of the New York *Tribune* and a veteran in the profession, delivered an eloquent and appropriate address, the concluding portion of which, for the sake of the craft so creditably represented in Mr. Colfax, and for the sake of its lesson to young men, we reproduce.

"Eighteen years ago, at one o'clock of a winter moonlighted morning, while the horses of the stage-coach in which I was plowing the thick mud of Indiana were being changed at the tavern in South Bend, I walked the footway of the principal street to shake off a great weariness. I saw a light through a window. A sign, *The Register*, was legible above it, and I saw through the window a man in his shirt sleeves walking quickly about like one that worked. I paused, and looked, and imagined about the man, and about his work, and about the lateness of the hour to which it was protracted, and I wondered if he was in debt and was struggling to get out, and if his wife was expecting him and had lighted a new candle for his coming, and if he was very tired. A coming step interrupted this idle dreaming. When the walker reached my side I joined him, and as we went I asked him questions, and naturally they were about the workman in his shirt sleeves. 'What sort of a man is he?' 'He is very good to the poor; he works hard; he is sociable with all people; he pays his debts; he is a safe adviser; he doesn't drink whisky; folks depend on him; all this part of Indiana believes in him.' From that day to this I have never taken up the South Bend *Register* without thinking of this eulogy and envying the man who had justly entitled himself to it in the dawn of his manhood. That man when 25 years of age, and again when 29 years old, was sent by his neighbors to the National Presidential Convention; when 27 years old was sent by his neighbors as a wise political reformer to the Constitutional Convention of the State of Indiana; was sent by the same neighbors to Congress in the year 1854, and kept there by them from that day to this. On the first Monday of this month of December the Republicans of the House of Representatives unanimously elected him Speaker of that body."

If Mr. Wilkeson had been gifted with a prophet's vision he would have seen in the near future the South Bend editor occupying a seat of still higher honor, the chair of the Vice President of the United States. But the verdict of the American people in 1868 had not then been revealed. Mr. Wilkeson concluded his address by attributing the success of Mr. Colfax largely to his kindness of heart and his broad philanthropy, first, however, paying a tribute to his fidelity to principle, his thorough attention to business, his talent for legislation, and the devotion of his gifts to the public good.

Eloquent and generous as was this eulogy there remains a very important element in the success of Schuyler Colfax which his graceful eulogist seems not to have observed. We allude to it more for the sake of its example to young men —its new reading of old proverbs—than from any desire to improve upon Mr. Wilkeson's words. Schuyler Colfax when a mere boy left his childhood's home in New York and went with his mother's family to the West. He found work and friends in South Bend, then a small town in the State of Indiana. He found also that there was room there for him to grow and become a useful citizen, and he resolved to make South Bend his future home. He became an editor. And South Bend continued to be his home until the day of his death. He did not remain there a year or two years and then become discouraged, abandon his office, and seek a new location, to be in turn abandoned for another and another. Not at all. *He stayed in South Bend; he stuck to his business;* and South Bend sent him to Congress over and over again. Its devotion to him made him Vice President when

Grant was President. As editor, Congressman, Speaker of the House, and Vice President it could truthfully be said that "folks depend on him." The whole nation trusted him.

There is no room for doubt that the success of this man whose name was long a household word in this country was due most of all to that trait in his character which led him to "settle down" for life in the community which had generously opened its arms to receive him and which held out to him the promise of a livelihood and of honors in accordance with his merits. It was a poetic and kindly thought in Mr. Wilkeson to ascribe the success of Schuyler Colfax largely to his broad philanthropy, but the philanthropist is not always rewarded in this world. Benevolence alone will not send any man to Congress. Schuyler Colfax succeeded because he joined to his generous character and his many talents the twin virtues of *persistence in a chosen occupation and contentment with his lot.*

The life of Schuyler Colfax teaches above all else this lesson to young men, the lesson of all human experience, that to be successful they must stick to one pursuit and stay in one place. If the life of any other successful man seems to teach a different lesson it should be remembered that extraordinary mental power and unusually favorable opportunities, which seldom fail to bring success anywhere, even when not combined, are themselves exceptions to a general rule. Schuyler Colfax was not a great man; he was a man of more industry than genius; nor were his early opportunities especially favorable; but he was one of the most successful public men in the history of his country, and he succeeded because he stayed in South Bend and stuck to his printing office.

# CHAPTER XXVIII.

## BUCKEYES IN AMERICAN HISTORY.

OHIO, the first of the States north of the Ohio river to be admitted into the Union, has furnished the country with a greater number of distinguished military leaders and civilians than any other State, Virginia alone excepted, and even the Old Dominion's race of great men belongs almost entirely to the Revolutionary period and to the period of the Rebellion. George H. Thomas, Joseph E. Johnston, Robert E. Lee, and Thomas J. Jackson, all heroes of the Rebellion period, but not all on the same side, were Virginians, and they were all great men. William Henry Harrison, William Wirt, Zachary Taylor, Winfield Scott, and Henry Clay form the only conspicuous links between Virginia's great men of the Revolutionary period and her great men of the Rebellion period. But William Wirt was born in Maryland, while Harrison early became identified with the development of the country north of the Ohio; Clay lived nearly all his days in Kentucky; and Taylor and Scott practically lost their identity with their native State after they entered the army. Since the surrender at Appomattox no son of Virginia has prominently come to the front in any sphere of human activity, military or civil. Not so, however, with Ohio. She began to produce great men, or at least distinguished men, as soon as she became a State in 1803, and she has not relaxed her efforts in this direction to the present time.

Of the twenty-five Presidents of the United States four have come from Ohio—William Henry Harrison, Hayes, Garfield, and McKinley, while two others, Grant and Benjamin Harrison, were natives of Ohio. The present Secretary of State, John Sherman, is a native of Ohio and was appointed from that State. Of the Secretaries of the Treasury five have come from Ohio—Ewing, Corwin, Chase, Sherman, and Foster, while Windom was a native of Ohio. Of the Secretaries of War Cass, although born in New Hampshire, was appointed from Ohio by Jackson and was subsequently Buchanan's Secretary of State, while Stanton, the greatest of our war ministers, was Ohio born, as is also General Alger, the present Secretary of War. Of the Postmaster Generals three have come from Ohio—Meigs, McLean, and Dennison. Of the Attorney Generals four have come from Ohio—Stanton, Stanberry, Taft, and Harmon. Of the Secretaries of the Interior, which department was not organized until 1849, three have come from Ohio—Ewing, Cox, and Delano, while Noble was born in Ohio. The first Secretary of Agriculture, Rusk, was born in Ohio. There have been only eight Chief Justices of the Supreme Court, and two of these, Chase and Waite, have come from Ohio, although natives of New England, while McLean and Swayne, of Ohio, were among the most noted Justices of that Court, although McLean was born in New Jersey and Swayne in Virginia. Joseph Warren Keifer, a native of Ohio and a Representative in Congress from that State, was the Speaker of the Forty-seventh Congress.

This list of prominent civilians contributed to the country by Ohio may be further extended by including the names of Wade, Giddings, and Thurman, none of whom, however, were born in Ohio. Two natives of Ohio, Schenck and McKinley, have given their names to important tariff bills, each having been chairman of the Committee on Ways and Means of the House of Representatives. Senator Allison, of Iowa, and Senator Elkins, of West Virginia, were born in Ohio, as were also Thomas A. Edison, the noted electrician, and Matthew Simpson, the eminent Methodist bishop.

The President and his Cabinet of eight ministers—nine in all—are usually designated as "The Administration." Of the late Harrison Administration (1889 to 1893) four of its members were born in Ohio—the President, and Secretaries Noble, Rusk, and Foster, the last named taking the place of Windom, who was also born in Ohio. President Cleveland found one of his Constitutional advisers in Ohio, Attorney General Harmon. President McKinley and his Secretary of State and Secretary of War are natives of Ohio, as has already been stated.

The prominence of Ohio in the military history of the country has been even more marked than its prominence in our civil affairs. William Henry Harrison was the hero of Tippecanoe and the battle of the Thames long before he became President. Lewis Cass distinguished himself as an officer in the second war with Great Britain before he became noted as a politician. The great triumvirate of the Union armies during the civil war—Grant, Sherman, and Sheridan —must all be credited to Ohio. They were all reared within its borders, and all were appointed cadets at West Point from that State, while two of the three, Grant and Sherman, were Ohio born. Sheridan was born at Albany, New York. McPherson, Custer, Rosecrans, McDowell, several of the fighting McCooks, and many other military leaders on the loyal side in the war for the Union were natives of Ohio. General O. M. Mitchel, the eminent astronomer, who also attained distinction as a soldier during the war for the Union, was a resident of Ohio from childhood, although a native of Kentucky. Hayes made a creditable record as a soldier before he became prominent as a politician, while Schenck was as prominent as a military man as he was as a civilian, and Garfield and McKinley were also soldiers.

Although a Western State, far removed from the "cultivation" of the East, Ohio is worthy of high honor as the mother of many prominent literary men and women. Our eminent American novelist, William Dean Howells, is a native of Ohio, and so is Whitelaw Reid, one of the most noted of American journalists. Reid made his reputation as a war correspondent, writing over the signature of "Agate." Murat Halstead, another American journalist of distinction, was born in Ohio and established his reputation while residing in his native State. Mrs. Harriet Beecher Stowe wrote *Uncle Tom's Cabin* after a long residence, from 1832 to 1850, at Cincinnati, where she became acquainted with the evils of negro slavery. The Cary sisters, who easily rank first among the female poets of America, were natives of Ohio. Albion W. Tourgee, author of *A Fool's Errand*, is a native of Ohio. Colonel William H. Lytle, the author of that notable poem which begins with the words, "I am dying, Egypt, dying," was a native of Ohio and a resident of that State all his days. David R. Locke, otherwise known as Petroleum V. Nasby, made his reputation as a humorist while editing the Toledo *Blade*, and Charles F. Browne, another humorist of national reputation, wrote his first letter over the signature of Artemus Ward while he was engaged as a reporter on an Ohio newspaper. Neither humorist was, however, a native of Ohio. Samuel S. Cox, who was long a prominent Representative in Congress, and who was best known by his sobriquet of "Sunset," was a native of Ohio. He was a prolific writer on both serious and humorous subjects.

The people of Ohio are often called Buckeyes, the name being given to them from the abundance of buckeyes, or horse chestnuts, among its native trees. One of the dialect poets of the day, James Whitcomb Riley, has written a "poem" about buckeyes, meaning the trees of that name and the nuts produced by them. He asks in bad grammar and answers the question, "What is buckeyes good for?" If he had asked the same question concerning the men and women of Ohio he could easily have found an answer in the history of the country's notable achievements in war and in peace.

# CHAPTER XXIX.

## OUR NEARNESS TO REVOLUTIONARY TIMES.

On the 30th day of April, 1789, George Washington was inaugurated at New York as the first President of the United States. From the Declaration of Independence, in 1776, until the important event above mentioned the thirteen United States which had previously been thirteen British colonies were held together chiefly by ties of common danger rather than by ties of mutual interest in peaceful pursuits. The political bonds that united them were of the lightest and most fragile character. But little respect was paid to them and but little help was expected from them. Each of the thirteen States was practically an independent republic. The Articles of Confederation, which were adopted in 1777, had failed to cement the rebellious colonies into a compact sovereignty. Those were the days of States' rights. It can scarcely be said that in those days we were a nation. The country was not prosperous, nor was it in the way of becoming strong and powerful. A new form of government became a necessity. Our present Constitution was framed in 1787, and in 1789, but little over one hundred years ago, it became fully operative with Washington's inauguration.

To those of us who have lived half a century and more it does not seem a very long time since Revolutionary days and the inauguration of Washington as our first President. A few persons are yet living who were born before he died in 1799. A larger number of persons are living to-day and are not yet very old men who have seen and talked with heroes of the Revolution—with men who had fought in its battles against the redcoats of George the Third. We can ourselves remember frequently seeing one of these heroes, Samuel Cole. The captain of a volunteer military company which fired a salute over the grave of the old soldier more than fifty years ago died as late as 1894.

Lafayette was the close friend and military adviser of Washington, yet many of our old friends who were recently living and some who are still living have seen and talked with this liberty-loving Frenchman when he paid a visit to our country in 1824 and 1825. One of these friends, who died in 1891, told us that he played the drum on the 3d day of June, 1825, upon the occasion of Lafayette's reception by the people of the town of Butler, Pennsylvania, and that the fifer whom he accompanied with his drum was a Revolutionary soldier, named Peter McKinney, who had played a fife at the battle of Bunker Hill, in 1775, just fifty years before. Lafayette was born in 1757 and lived until 1834.

William Henry Harrison knew Washington personally. He was twenty-six years old when the Father of his Country died, and yet there are many of our countrymen still living who knew the hero of Tippecanoe intimately, while thousands of persons are living who voted for him for President in 1836 and 1840. Washington was the friend of Benjamin Harrison, the father of William Henry Harrison, and it was with the assistance of Washington that the young man entered the army as an ensign in 1791.

Robert C. Winthrop was born in 1809 and died in 1894. He was Speaker of the House of Representatives from 1847 to 1849. In 1848 he witnessed the death of John Quincy

Adams, sixth President of the United States, who was born in 1767. Mr. Adams shared as a boy the hopes and fears of the Revolutionary struggle, and at its close he assisted his father as secretary in drafting in 1783 the treaty of peace which established our independence. Mr. Winthrop could have told any of the readers of this paragraph down to the year of his own death what Mr. Adams had told him of his personal recollections of the Revolution and of Revolutionary leaders. Andrew Jackson, who died in 1845, and who received the votes of persons who are yet living when he was a Presidential candidate in 1824 and 1828, and of a larger number when he was a candidate in 1832, was born in 1767, the same year in which Mr. Adams was born. He must have communicated to many of our cotemporaries his boyish recollections of the times that tried men's souls.

But Mr. Winthrop had talked with even older men than John Quincy Adams. In 1832, when returning from a visit to James Madison, he saw at his own house in Baltimore Charles Carroll, of Carrollton, the last surviving signer of the Declaration of Independence, who was born in 1737 and died in 1832; and in 1837 he visited at Stratham, New Hampshire, Paine Wingate, the last surviving member of the first Senate of the United States, then in his 99th year, who was born in 1739 and who had dined with Washington in 1789 on the day of his first inauguration. He died in 1838.

Justin S. Morrill, who has long honored and still honors the State of Vermont as one of its representatives in the United States Senate, tells us that when he was eight years old he saw President James Monroe at Strafford, Vermont, in 1818. James Monroe was born in 1758 and was a soldier in the Revolution. Mr. Morrill also tells us that on the 4th day of July, 1831, he called on John Quincy Adams at his home in Quincy, Massachusetts, and that on the same day he heard him deliver an oration, appropriate to the day, at a church in Quincy. Mr. Morrill afterwards saw Mr. Adams at Washington when the ex-President was a member of the House of Representatives. Elijah Paine, who was born in 1757, was a United States Senator from Vermont from 1795 to 1801, taking his seat when Washington was still President, over a hundred years ago, and from 1801 to 1842 he was Judge of the United States District Court of Vermont, dying in the latter year. Mr. Morrill often saw Judge Paine, who was always dressed in the old Continental style. He always called himself one of John Adams's "midnight judges," having been appointed by Adams on the last day of his Presidential term. It seems to us to be a most interesting fact that a member of the present Senate of the United States should have seen and talked with a gentleman who was a United States Senator when Washington was President.

Henry C. Carey is well known to this generation as our greatest political economist. He was born in Philadelphia in 1793 and died in 1879, in his 86th year. We knew him well and never saw a handsomer old man. In his later years he was a frequent visitor to our office in Philadelphia. He was six years old when Washington died. When a young man he had seen and talked with many of the Revolutionary heroes. Deborah Fisher Wharton, a prominent member of the Society of Friends, who was born in Philadelphia in 1795 and who died in 1888, remembered seeing Washington when she was a child and he was pointed out to her on the street. Mrs. Wharton was the mother of Joseph

Wharton. On the same square on which our office is located lived Horace Binney for many years prior to his death in 1875, at the age of 95 years. He was born in Philadelphia in 1780, before the struggle with Great Britain had ended. We also knew this venerable man. He was nineteen years old when Washington died, and, living in Philadelphia all his days, he must have seen him frequently when he was President, as well as many other heroes of the Revolutionary period, Franklin included, who died in 1790.

The venerable Frederick Fraley, of Philadelphia, who is now (1897) in his 94th year, having been born in Philadelphia in May, 1804, tells us that his father, John U. Fraley, who was born in 1776, frequently saw Washington. Pointing to a portrait of Washington one day he told his son "Fred" that Washington looked like that portrait. Mr. Fraley's recollection is that the portrait very closely resembled Stuart's celebrated painting. Mr. Fraley also tells us that in 1817, precisely eighty years ago, when he was himself thirteen years old, he was present at the laying of the corner-stone of the Bridesburg Arsenal, in Philadelphia, when President James Monroe, at whose side he was standing, asked him to give the stone three taps with a wooden mallet, which he did, the President himself having just performed the same act as a part of the corner-stone ceremonial. Mr. Fraley has seen every President since Monroe. He also saw Lafayette in 1824, and a few years later he escorted Chief Justice John Marshall through the fair of the Franklin Institute of Philadelphia. Marshall was born in 1755 and died in 1835. Mr. Fraley was a delegate to the National Whig Convention at Harrisburg in 1839 which nominated William Henry Harrison for the Presidency.

Richard W. Thompson, of Terre Haute, who was born in 1809 and is now in his 89th year, has recently published his personal recollections, in which he states that he has seen all the Presidents except Washington and John Adams. He describes minutely the personal appearance of Jefferson, who was born in 1743, and of Madison, who was born in 1749.

At the end of a little over a hundred years we are not, therefore, very far removed from Washington's inauguration or from the days of the Revolution itself. It is not yet a hundred years since Washington died. Viewed through the memories which connect us with Revolutionary days this is still a new country and we are still a new people. It is only when we turn to the events and the traditions of "good old colony times," and particularly before the days "when George the Third was King," his accession to the throne taking place in 1760, that we begin to realize how widely we are separated from the pioneers whose thin and scattered settlements along the Atlantic coast were the first steps that were taken in making us a nation.

And yet it is possible even now to be brought into close touch with colonial times. Mr. Blaine once told us that when he was a boy he knew an old man who told him that when himself a boy he had known an old man who had witnessed the coronation of Queen Anne in 1702, nearly two hundred years ago. Benjamin Franklin was born four years later, in 1706, and lived until 1790. The old men who are still living and have talked with Washington's compatriots may have received from them their personal recollections of Franklin. Charles Carroll and Paine Wingate must have communicated to men who are still living their recollections of the days long before the Revolution.

## OUR NEARNESS TO REVOLUTIONARY TIMES.

In closing this retrospect of colonial and Revolutionary times we wish to emphasize the full significance of the facts we have stated concerning some of our fellow citizens who are still living. Frederick Fraley can describe the personal appearance of John Marshall, who was born in 1755, of Lafayette, who was born in 1757, and of Monroe, who was born in 1758, and Senator Morrill can also describe the personal appearance of Monroe and of Judge Paine, the latter having been born in 1757. It is a long way back to the sixth decade of the eighteenth century, a hundred and forty years ago. Still more remarkable are the reminiscences of Mr. Thompson, who describes for us the personal appearance of Jefferson and Madison, who were born in the fifth decade of the eighteenth century, a hundred and fifty years ago.

# CHAPTER XXX.

#### HONORING THE MIGHTY DEAD.

The address of the Honorable Edward J. Phelps, at the dedication of the battle monument at Bennington, Vermont, on August 19, 1891, was unquestionably one of the most perfect of its kind that has ever been delivered before an American audience. The concluding part of it, which embodies the orator's tribute to Vermont, and which describes the inspiring lesson of patriotism and virtue that the magnificent monument will teach to coming generations, is worthy of preservation as an American classic of the highest order. In this masterly address our late Minister to England has won for the Green Mountain State a new honor which she can now add to all the other honors that have been heaped upon her. He has shown that she possesses a great orator, who has fitly and gracefully and fervently recorded the great deeds of her mighty dead.

The mighty dead of all the States! Is there a nation in the world that honors the memory of its great men, whether statesmen or soldiers, men of letters or men of action, as this young nation honors those who have placed it in the front of all the nations? From the death of Washington in 1799 to the death of Sherman in 1891 how general has been the regret, how unstinted has been the praise, when a great man has fallen among us! Especially since the close of our civil war, more than a quarter of a century ago, have we shown a veneration for the illustrious deeds of our countrymen in every period of our history that will well compare in sincerity and intensity with the honors which the people of other countries, ancient and modern, have paid to the memory of their heroes and sages. The centennial anniversaries of Revolutionary events, uniting with the growing appreciation of the heroic achievements of the civil war, have deepened in the breast of every loyal American the feeling of respect and gratitude which we instinctively cherish for those who have well served their country in field or forum, or conspicuously advanced in any way its prosperity and glory. The battle monument at Bennington is the last of the Revolutionary memorials that the gratitude of a great people has erected. It will be followed by others commemorating great events and honoring great actors in peace and in war in every period of our eventful history, until the land will be dotted with statues and the heavens in every part of the horizon will be pierced with shafts of granite and marble. Our great wealth will make possible in a short time that which other countries have been ages in accomplishing.

But we honor our mighty dead and teach the lesson of their useful lives in other ways than with statues and monuments. Our observance of the 4th of July, the 22d of February, and the 8th of January shows our grateful remembrance of the men who participated in the important events of the early days of the Republic, while the growing tendency to honor the birthdays of Lincoln and Grant shows that these great men have taken their place with Washington and his compatriots in the hearts of all true Americans. Memorial Day tells of our gratitude to the private soldier of the civil war, and our long pension roll tells of our care for himself and his family. The bank notes issued by the Government are stamped with the lineaments of many among our dead who have been eminent in our military and civil annals.

The formal eulogy by set speech of the character and services of a great citizen who has departed is a custom of the ancients which is so much observed in our country that we look for it as a matter of course. Rarely is this custom neglected. When a member of Congress dies it is always observed, although many deceased members of Congress have been in no way distinguished. When Washington, Jefferson, the first Adams, William Henry Harrison, Jackson, Taylor, Clay, and Webster died formal eulogies were pronounced in many places. When Lincoln and Garfield and Grant died every pulpit in the land expressed the sorrow of the whole American people. In memory of Lincoln and Garfield the most imposing services were held in the Hall of the House of Representatives at Washington. We never could understand why similar services were not held in the same place when Congress met after the death of Grant. It was a great blunder. But it was no greater than that of President Cleveland, who did not even refer to the death of his illustrious predecessor in his annual message to Congress after that sad event had shocked a grateful country. But these are exceptions to the general rule.

Looking over some notable eulogies which are in our library, published by authority of Congress, we are impressed first by their general literary excellence and next by the uniform absence of all partisan feeling in their preparation. We have before us Bancroft's eulogy of Lincoln and Blaine's eulogy of Garfield, each eulogy having been delivered in the Hall of the House of Representatives at the request of both houses of Congress. Here, too, are the Congressional eulogies of Thaddeus Stevens, John Covode, Dudley C. Haskell, William D. Kelley, and Samuel J. Randall —all dying in Congressional harness. Worthier tribunes of the people than these members of the House this country has not produced. All of them unselfishly devoted their great talents and their tireless energies to their country's welfare, and there can be no doubt that the death of at least one of these great men was hastened by that devotion. This country is rich in the names of public servants who have won distinction caring for its interests as these great men did, and these other great men are not forgotten.

Bancroft's eulogy of Lincoln and Blaine's eulogy of Garfield are productions of unequal merit. Bancroft had the greater subject and he was wholly unequal to it. Blaine's eulogy of Garfield is a masterpiece. Bancroft's address is mainly a political essay, dealing with the remote causes of the war for the Union rather than with the war itself, and it contains a most meagre and unsatisfactory analysis of Lincoln's great character, which he plainly did not understand, as, for instance, where he says that Lincoln "excelled in logical statement *more than in executive ability.*" He excelled in both. The distinguished orator could think of no more felicitous way of glorifying Lincoln than by favorably comparing him with Lord Palmerston, the British Prime Minister, who had just died, and who is not worthy to be mentioned in the same day with Lincoln. The address is turgid in style, and it is sadly marred by reference to the orator's own opinions and personal griefs. Horace Greeley's more recently published tribute to Lincoln in the *Century Magazine* far excels that of our great historian. Bancroft's closing words, which, with singular inappropriateness, did not forget himself, were tamely as follows:

"Senators and Representatives of America: As I bid you farewell my last words shall be words of hope and confidence; for now slavery is no more, the Union is restored, a people begins to live according to the laws of reason, and republicanism is intrenched in a continent."

Blaine's eulogy of Garfield is not so retrospective and philosophic as that of Bancroft, but it is more happily conceived and is what a funeral oration should be—an account of the life and public services of the dead soldier or civilian in whose honor it is delivered. The influences which had moulded Lincoln's character, his family history, his early privations, were all touched upon by Bancroft, but Blaine dwelt upon Garfield's ancestry and his early life with greater sympathy and greater felicity. Bancroft did not idealize his hero as much as he should have done and would have been justified in doing. Blaine checked with judicious but ample words the extravagant praise of Garfield that would then have been excused but would not have been merited. His analysis of Garfield's mental qualities and religious professions is clear and in good taste. Mr. Blaine was conspicuously a man of letters and of literary accomplishments. We may well regret that the task which fell to Bancroft in 1866 had not fallen to the young and rising statesman from Maine. Although a member of Garfield's Cabinet, and although Garfield was struck down at his side, Blaine never refers to himself in his whole address. The peroration forms one of the most eloquent and poetic and pathetic passages in the English language. We give it in full below.

"As the end drew near his early craving for the sea returned. The stately mansion of power had been to him the wearisome hospital of pain, and he begged to be taken from its prison walls, from its oppressive, stifling air, from its homelessness and its hopelessness. Gently, silently, the love of a great people bore the pale sufferer to the longed-for healing of the sea, to live or to die, as God should will, within sight of its heaving billows, within sound of its manifold voices. With wan, fevered face, tenderly lifted to the cooling breeze, he looked out wistfully upon the ocean's changing wonders; on its fair sails, whitening in the morning light; on its restless waves, rolling shoreward to break and die beneath the noonday sun; on the red clouds of evening, arching low to the horizon; on the serene and shining pathway of the stars. Let us think that his dying eyes read a mystic meaning which only the rapt and parting soul may know. Let us believe that in the silence of the receding world he heard the great waves breaking on a farther shore, and felt already upon his wasted brow the breath of the eternal morning."

Thoughtful people must always regret that the memory of Grant was not so promptly, conspicuously, and appropriately honored as that of Lincoln and Garfield. The display at the dedication of his tomb at Riverside, in 1897, twelve years after his death, atoned only in part for this neglect. No orator and no essayist has yet done justice to the character and services of this great man. On Thursday, August 20, 1890, at Mt. McGregor, New York, where Grant died in 1885, President Harrison made the happiest reference to the dead hero that has yet been made anywhere. He said: "It has been said that a great life went out here; but great lives, like that of General Grant, do not go out. *They go on.*"

# PERSONAL INDEX.

| | Page |
|---|---|
| Acrelius, Israel | 140 |
| Adams, John | 70, 214, 216, 220 |
| Adams, John Quincy | 213, 214 |
| Albert, George Dallas | 176 |
| Alger, General Russell A. | 207 |
| Allen, Colonel Ethan | 137 |
| Allen, Zachariah | 110 |
| Allison, William B. | 100, 208 |
| Anne, Queen | 216 |
| Anshutz, George | 175 |
| Anthony, Richard | 110 |
| Appleton, William | 110 |
| Argyll, Duke of | 31 |
| Arthur, Chester A. | 97, 116 |
| Ashe, Thomas | 171 |
| Ashton, John | 41 |
| Bailey, Mr. (Welsh ironmaster) | 44 |
| Bancroft, George | 1, 139, 220, 221, 222 |
| Bates, Theodore C. | 115 |
| Besant, Annie | 45 |
| Besant, Walter | 44 |
| Bigelow, Erastus B. | 17 |
| Binney, Horace | 215 |
| Bishop, Dr. J. Leander | 74 |
| Blackstone, Sir William | 8, 12, 14 |
| Blaine, James G. | 58, 71, 93, 94, 114, 196, 199, 202, 216, 220, 221, 222 |
| Booth, James C. | 151 |
| Booth, General William | 46 |
| Borie, John J. | 110 |
| Bouquet, Colonel Henry | 169, 170 |
| Bowen, Professor Francis | 86, 87 |
| Braddock, General Edward | 169 |
| Brassey, Thomas | 27 |
| Brewer, J. Hart | 115 |
| Bright, John | 33, 49, 50 |
| Britton, J. Blodget | 152 |
| Brooke, Rev. Stopford | 46 |
| Brougham, Lord | 1, 73 |

| | Page |
|---|---|
| Brown, Edward | 152 |
| Browne, Charles F. | 209 |
| Buchanan, James | 75, 79, 90, 92, 207 |
| Burke, Edmund | 55 |
| Burnett, John | 88 |
| Butler, General Benjamin F. | 95 |
| Byles, Sir John Barnard | 28, 29, 36, 54, 56 |
| Carey, Henry C. | 18, 92, 113, 132, 214 |
| Carey, Mathew | 107, 108, 109, 110 |
| Carlisle, John G. | 97, 98, 99, 125, 126 |
| Carnegie, Andrew | 176 |
| Carroll, Charles, of Carrollton | 213, 216 |
| Cary, Phœbe and Alice | 209 |
| Cass, Lewis | 207, 208 |
| Chambers, Thomas | 112 |
| Chapman, T. J. | 176 |
| Charles I. | 30, 54 |
| Charles II. | 11, 12, 16 |
| Chase, Salmon P. | 207 |
| Chatham, Lord | 15 |
| Clay, Henry | 2, 75, 76, 77, 78, 80, 107, 111, 206, 220 |
| Cleveland, Grover | 80, 98, 99, 100, 101, 102, 129, 130, 182, 208, 220 |
| Cobbett, William | 56 |
| Cobden, Richard | 49, 50, 51 |
| Coleman, Dr. L. H. | 75 |
| Colfax, Schuyler | 202, 204, 205 |
| Colwell, Stephen | 113 |
| Converse, George L. | 98 |
| Cooke, Jay | 80 |
| Cooper & Hewitt | 84, 85, 113 |
| Cooper, James M. | 117 |
| Cooper, Peter | 84, 114 |
| Corning, Gurdon | 110 |
| Corwin, Thomas | 207 |
| Covert, James W. | 95, 96 |
| Covode, John | 221 |

## PERSONAL INDEX.

Cowan, Christopher....................... 175
Cox, Jacob D................................. 207
Cox, Samuel S.............................. 210
Craig, Major Isaac....................... 170
Craig, Neville B..................... 171, 176
Craig & O'Hara............................. 174
Crawford, Thomas H..................... 76
Crisp, Charles F............................ 102
Cromwell, Oliver........................... 11
Cunard, Samuel....................... 65, 66
Custer, General George A............. 208

Dallas, George M.......................... 78
Dalzell, John................................. 108
Davidson, Professor Thomas......... 23
Davis, Jefferson............................. 53
Davis, John................................... 77
Dawes, Henry L............................ 94
Delano, Columbus.................. 114, 207
Dennison, William......................... 207
Dingley, Nelson, Jr....................... 105
Dinwiddie, Governor Robert.. 167, 168
Disraeli, Benjamin........................ 44
Dixon, Nathan F............................ 110
Dobson, James.............................. 114
Dodge, William E..................... 40, 41
Durfee, William F......................... 151

Eckert, George N........................... 116
Ecuyer, Captain Simeon................ 170
Edison, Thomas A.......................... 208
Edward III................................... 8, 9
Edward IV..................................... 8
Elder, Cyrus............................ 115, 116
Elder, Dr. William.................... 14, 19
Elizabeth, Queen..... 3, 7, 9, 10, 12, 54
Elkins, Stephen B.......................... 208
Everett, Alexander H.............. 110, 111
Ewing, Thomas........................ 109, 207

Fillmore, Millard........................... 89
Fraley, Frederick.................... 215, 217
Francis, Colonel............................ 173
Franklin, Benjamin... 70, 137, 215, 216
Forbes, General John............... 169, 171
Forward, Walter...................... 109, 110
Foster, Charles....................... 207, 208
Frick, Henry C.............................. 176

Gage, General Thomas.................. 170

Gallatin, Albert............................. 111
Garfield, James A.......... 207, 209, 220
........................................ 221, 222, 223
Garfield, Samuel........................... 110
Geary, Governor John W............... 166
Geary, Richard.............................. 166
George I................................... 12, 13
George II.................................. 13, 15
George III...................... 13, 212, 216
Giddings, Joshua R....................... 207
Gladstone, William E. 28, 48, 49, 53, 60
Gorman, Arthur P.......................... 103
Granger, Francis............................ 109
Grant, General U. S....... 205, 207, 208
........................................ 219, 220, 223
Greeley, Horace...................... 115, 221
Greene, General Nathanael........... 137
Grinnell, James B.......................... 115
Guthrie, James......................... 79, 125

Haldeman, James M...................... 110
Hallam, Henry.............................. 7
Halstead, Murat............................ 209
Hamilton, Alexander........ 70, 71, 107
........................................ 108, 148
Harmon, Judson...................... 207, 208
Harrison, Benjamin......... 99, 196, 198
........................................ 207, 223
Harrison, Benjamin (Signer)......... 212
Harrison, William Henry...... 206, 207
.............................. 208, 212, 215, 220
Haskell, Dudley C......................... 221
Hayes, John L............................... 97
Hayes, Rutherford B.............. 207, 209
Henry VIII............................ 9, 10, 54
Hewitt, Abram S.. 84, 85, 113, 117, 153
Hite, A. J...................................... 162
Hoar, Samuel................................ 110
Holliday, John........................ 163, 165
Howell, Benjamin B...................... 110
Howells, William Dean................. 209
Huskisson, William....................... 32
Huxley, Professor Thomas H........ 32

Ingersoll, Charles J....................... 109
Irvin, General James..................... 116

Jackson, Andrew.. 75, 99, 207, 213, 220
Jackson, General Thomas J.......... 206
Jarrett, John.................................. 115

## PERSONAL INDEX.

| Name | Page |
|---|---|
| Jefferson, Thomas | 70, 108, 111, 217, 220 |
| Johnson, Edward T | 115 |
| Johnston, General Joseph E | 206 |
| Jones, A. H | 115 |
| Jones, A. M | 110 |
| Jones, B. F | 114, 176 |
| Jones, John P | 71 |
| Kay, Joseph | 29, 30, 43, 44 |
| Keifer, Joseph Warren | 97, 207 |
| Kelley, William D | 11, 65, 91, 96, 97, 99, 114, 115, 221 |
| Kennedy, John P | 110 |
| Kerr, Michael C | 95, 154 |
| Kingsley, Charles | 49, 50 |
| Lafayette, Marquis de | 212, 215, 217 |
| Lamborn, Robert H | 117 |
| Lawrence, Abbott | 109, 110 |
| Lee, Arthur | 172 |
| Lee, General Robert E | 206 |
| Lesley, Professor J. P | 116 |
| Lewis, Ellis | 110 |
| Lincoln, Abraham | 80, 99, 137, 176, 219, 220, 221, 223 |
| Lincoln, Daniel | 137 |
| Lincoln, Mordecai | 137 |
| Livingston, Peter R | 110 |
| Locke, David R | 209 |
| Loring, George B | 114 |
| Lytle, Colonel William H | 209 |
| Mac Carthy, (Commissioner) | 54, 55 |
| Macpherson, (Annals of Commerce) | 4 |
| McClurg, Joseph | 175 |
| McCooks | 208 |
| McCulloch, (Commercial Dictionary) | 15, 17 |
| McDowell, General Irvin | 208 |
| McKay, Nathaniel | 38 |
| McKinley, William | 49, 50, 82, 100, 105, 114, 207, 208, 209 |
| McLean, John | 207 |
| McPherson, General James B | 208 |
| Madison, James | 70, 71, 99, 111, 213, 216, 217 |
| Mallary, Rollin C | 109 |
| Manning, Cardinal | 50 |
| Marshall, John | 215, 217 |
| Marshall, Samuel S | 154 |
| Mary, Queen | 7 |
| Meagher, Thomas Francis | 59 |
| Meigs, Return J | 207 |
| Merrick, S. V | 110 |
| Miller, Warner | 114 |
| Mills, Roger Q | 98, 99 |
| Mitchel, General O. M | 209 |
| Monroe, James | 213, 215, 217 |
| Morrell, Charles H | 110 |
| Morrill, Justin S | 92, 201, 213, 214, 217 |
| Morrison, William R | 95, 96, 97, 98 |
| Napier, Lord | 31 |
| Nasby, Petroleum V | 209 |
| Niles, Hezekiah | 110 |
| Noble, John | 34 |
| Noble, John W | 207, 208 |
| Paine, Elijah | 214, 217 |
| Palmerston, Lord | 221 |
| Parnell, Sir Henry | 20 |
| Parsons, W. J | 85 |
| Patterson, General Robert | 75 |
| Penn, John | 173 |
| Penn, Thomas | 173 |
| Peto, Sir S. Morton | 83 |
| Phelps, Edward J | 218 |
| Pierce, Franklin | 90, 180 |
| Pitkin, Timothy | 137, 139 |
| Pitt, William | 169 |
| Polk, James K | 78, 83 |
| Post, Christian Frederick | 171 |
| Proctor, Isaac | 161, 162, 163, 164, 165, 166 |
| Prosser, Colonel William F | 68 |
| Quay, Matthew S | 101, 103 |
| Rahm & Bean | 165 |
| Randall, Samuel J | 94, 95, 98, 99, 221 |
| Reed, Thomas B | 100, 105 |
| Reeves, Benjamin | 110 |
| Reeves, David | 110 |
| Reeves, Samuel J | 117 |
| Reid, Whitelaw | 209 |
| Ricketson, John H | 114 |
| Riley, James Whitcomb | 210 |
| Ritner, Joseph | 109 |
| Roach, John | 65, 66, 115 |
| Robbins, Ashur | 109 |

## PERSONAL INDEX.

| Name | Page |
|---|---|
| Roberts, Jonathan | 110 |
| Robinson, Mr. (member of Parliament) | 2 |
| Rodgers, James | 112 |
| Rodgers, Thomas | 110 |
| Rogers, Professor J. E. Thorold | 34 |
| Rosecrans, General W. S. | 208 |
| Rusk, Jeremiah M. | 207, 208 |
| Ruskin, John | 45 |
| Schenck, General Robert C. | 93, 94, 208 |
| Scott, John | 94 |
| Scott, General Winfield | 180, 206 |
| Scranton, Joseph H. | 117 |
| Scriven, Colonel John | 115 |
| Scrivenor, (History of the Iron Trade) | 19 |
| Seward, Asabel | 110 |
| Shaftesbury, Lord | 38, 39 |
| Shaler, Charles | 112 |
| Shallenberger, W. S. | 115 |
| Shaw-Lefevre, Mr. | 28 |
| Sheffield, Lord | 1 |
| Sheridan, General Philip H. | 208 |
| Sherman, John | 81, 102, 207 |
| Sherman, General W. T. | 208, 218 |
| Shoenberger, Dr. Peter | 164 |
| Shunk, Francis R. | 78 |
| Simmons, James F. | 110 |
| Simpson, Matthew | 208 |
| Smith, Charles E. | 113, 116 |
| Smith, Wellington | 115 |
| Stanberry, Henry | 207 |
| Stanton, Edwin M. | 207 |
| Stanwix, General John | 169 |
| Stebbins, Giles B. | 115 |
| Stevens, Thaddeus | 221 |
| Stewart, Andrew | 76, 112 |
| Stewart, John and Mathew | 175 |
| Stowe, Harriet Beecher | 209 |
| Sullivan, Sir Edward | 34 |
| Swayne, Noah H. | 207 |
| Swift, Dean | 55 |
| Taft, Alphonso | 207 |
| Tallmadge, James | 110 |
| Taylor, General Richard | 119 |
| Taylor, Zachary | 206, 220 |
| Thomas, David | 145 |
| Thomas, General George H. | 206 |
| Thompson, Richard W. | 216, 217 |
| Thompson, Robert Ellis | 16, 59 |
| Thurman, Allen G. | 207 |
| Tilghman, Mr. | 174 |
| Tillman, George D. | 118 |
| Tod, John | 74 |
| Tourgee, Albion W. | 209 |
| Towne, John H. | 116 |
| Trent, Captain William | 168 |
| Tyler, John | 83 |
| Victoria, Queen | 22, 23, 24, 29, 34, 36, 42, 43, 44, 46, 48, 49, 51, 53, 61 |
| Voorhees, Daniel W. | 102 |
| Wade, Benjamin F. | 207 |
| Waite, Morrison R. | 207 |
| Walker, Robert J. | 78, 83, 84 |
| Wallace, Edward | 80 |
| Ward, Artemus | 209 |
| Ward, Captain E. B. | 117 |
| Washington, Augustine | 137, 167 |
| Washington, George | 70, 71, 137, 167, 168, 169, 171, 172, 211, 212, 213, 214, 215, 216, 218, 220 |
| Washington, Lawrence | 167 |
| Waugh, Rev. Benjamin | 42 |
| Wayne, General Anthony | 171 |
| Webster, Daniel | 70, 220 |
| Webster, Ezekiel | 109 |
| Welles, Gideon | 109 |
| Wetherill, J. P. | 110 |
| Wharton, Deborah Fisher | 214 |
| Wharton, Joseph | 114, 115, 215 |
| Wheeler, Charles | 117 |
| Wilkeson, Samuel | 202, 204, 205 |
| Wilkins, William | 110 |
| William III | 12, 14, 54, 55 |
| Wilson, William L. | 81, 102 |
| Windom, William | 207 |
| Wingate, Paine | 213, 216 |
| Winthrop, Robert C. | 212, 213 |
| Wirt, William | 206 |
| Wood, Charles S. | 117 |
| Wood, Fernando | 95 |
| Young, Dr. Edward | 35 |
| Zincke, F. Barham | 31 |

www.ingramcontent.com/pod-product-compliance
Lightning Source LLC
Chambersburg PA
CBHW031746230426
43669CB00007B/506